Going Places 2

Picture-Based English

Teacher's Resource Book

Lois Maharg

Longman

Going Places: Picture-Based English, Teacher's Resource Book 2

A Publication of World Language Division

Associated companies:
Longman Group Ltd., London
Longman Cheshire Pty., Melbourne
Longman Paul Pty., Auckland
Copp Clark Pitman, Toronto

Editorial Director: Joanne Dresner
Acquisitions Editor: Anne Boynton-Trigg
Development Editor: Karen Davy
Consulting Editor: Michael Rost
Project Manager: Helen B. Ambrosio
Text Design Adaptation: Pencil Point Studio

ISBN: 0-201-82536-8

1 2 3 4 5 6 7 8 9 10-CRS-99 98 97 96 95

CONTENTS

Introduction

Going Places: Picture-Based English is a complete two-level course for beginning ESL students. It is designed to help students develop the practical language they need to function effectively at work, in the community, and in their personal lives. Going Places 2 consists of a fully illustrated Student Book, classroom audio cassettes, and a Teacher's Resource Book. The Student Book includes 28 units based on a carefully organized syllabus that integrates topical, life skill, and grammatical strands. The gradual progression of structural elements combined with the unique presentation of practical vocabulary make Going Places the ideal course for students beginning their study of English. Going Places features:

- pictures *without captions* as a vehicle for introducing and practicing new language

- integration of language structures and functional vocabulary within life skill contexts such as shopping, health care, and housing

- development of and practice in the four language skill areas of listening, speaking, reading, and writing, progressing in emphasis from reception to production

- opportunities for meaningful, personalized communication using newly acquired language

- lessons that engage students in pair practice and small-group interaction

- careful recycling of vocabulary and grammar throughout the book

- a broad range of activities that address various learning styles

- a cultural component in every lesson designed to heighten students' cross-cultural awareness.

The Student Book

Each unit in Going Places 2 follows a consistent format and is taught in three stages. The units begin with the presentation of vocabulary. The key to the successful presentation of vocabulary is to create a natural, personal interaction between teacher and students. Specific questions and sample presentations which help create this natural, personal interaction are provided in the Teacher's Notes at the back of the Student Book.

Presentation of vocabulary is followed by conversation practice in which students practice the new vocabulary and key grammatical structures. Much of the conversation practice is personalized, with students sharing information about themselves with partners.

The expansion activities in Going Places 2 help students achieve life skill competencies through listening, speaking, reading, and writing practice. They reinforce the grammatical focus of the unit, review and expand the vocabulary, and further personalize the language students have learned.

The Teacher's Resource Book

The Teacher's Resource Book provides step-by-step procedures for key exercises that recur frequently throughout the Student Book. For each unit of the Student Book, the Teacher's Resource Book features:

- detailed teaching suggestions that help teachers introduce new language structures and prepare students to perform tasks successfully

- sample language presentations for introducing the vocabulary

- recommendations for using selected activities to teach basic aspects of pronunciation, intonation, rhythm, and stress

- expansion activities that reinforce the grammar, vocabulary, and life skill components of each unit and challenge students to use the new language in less structured contexts

- reproducible grammar and reading-comprehension exercises.

Procedures for Key Exercises

Presentation of Vocabulary through Pictures

1. Direct students' attention to an overhead transparency of the pictures on the first page of each unit. If an overhead projector is not available, have students look at the first page of the unit—*not* the second page—in their books.

2. For each unit, refer to Activity 1 under the Teaching Suggestions in the Teacher's Resource Book, or turn to the Teacher's Notes in the Student Book, and ask students a series of yes/no and choice questions relating to each picture. For example: *Is there a library at our school?; Can you buy books in a library or a bookstore?*

3. Use simple language to ask the questions, and personalize the new vocabulary by asking questions that relate to students' lives.

4. When necessary, do the following to help students understand and answer your questions.

   a. Use pantomime.

   b. Point to clues in the pictures.

   c. Use "give-away" questions. For example: "Is this a *dog* or a *check*?"

   d. Simply feed students answers. For example: "Who has a checking account?…[No answer.] Peter, do you have a checkbook? [showing Peter a checkbook—Peter nods]…Yes, Peter has a checkbook. Then Peter has a checking account. Who else?…"

5. Use each new vocabulary item in several questions as you present it. Also, skip around the page and review frequently. For example: *Which picture has the ___[computers]___?; Point to the picture of the ___[vending machine]___.*

6. Have students keep their pencils down and notebooks closed during the presentation to keep their focus on the *oral* interaction. To give students a brief "visual take" on the new vocabulary items, write new words on the chalkboard as they are introduced and then quickly erase them.

Reinforcement of Vocabulary with Written Cues

The second page of each unit contains pictures from the opening page with captions.

1. Model the vocabulary items one by one and have students repeat them.

2. Certain items may require clarification as students are scrutinizing the target vocabulary in print. Answer any questions that arise.

3. Do the pairwork.

    a. First, model the task. Designate yourself as Student A and one of the more capable students as Student B. Have Student B turn to the first page of the unit and hold up his or her book for the rest of the class to see. Hold up your book so that the class sees you're looking at the second page of the unit.

    b. Say the vocabulary items aloud in random order as Student B points to the appropriate pictures, holding up his or her book to show the class.

    c. Put students in pairs, designating one as Student A and the other as Student B. Tell the A's to look at the second page of the unit and the B's to look at the first page. Tell the A's to say the vocabulary items and the B's to point to the appropriate pictures.

    d. As students are doing the pairwork, circulate to make sure they understand the task and to answer any questions.

    e. Have students switch roles for further practice.

Listen and Write

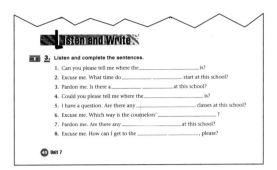

1. Put on the tape and play the instructions and item number 1.

2. Stop the tape. Check to see that students are doing the task correctly by asking what word or phrase they've written in the blank and writing it on the chalkboard. If necessary, play the first item again to verify the accuracy of the response.

3. Continue playing the tape until the end of the exercise. As students listen and write, they may be looking at the words at the top of the page. Do not discourage this. Students cannot be expected to have mastered the spelling of the new vocabulary items yet. If the task is difficult for your class, play the tape a second time.

4. Check students' responses in one of the following ways.

   a. Have individual students read the items aloud, completing the sentences with the words they've written in the blanks. Write the key words on the chalkboard.

   b. Have individual students write the missing words on the chalkboard.

5. Verify the accuracy of students' answers by playing the tape again, stopping it after each item and asking *Is it right?*

Grammar Box

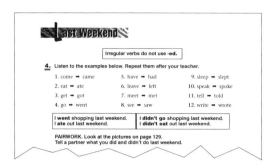

1. Write the material from the grammar box on the chalkboard.

2. Call students' attention to the element of structure being introduced. (This element is often highlighted.) Offer simple explanations of the structural element. For example: *Irregular verbs, such as go, do not use –ed.*

   Clarify the structures and answer questions as needed, but avoid lengthy explanations.

3. Engage students in an activity that enables them to practice the new structure in an immediate and personalized context. Ideas for such activities are provided in the Teaching Suggestions for each unit.

4. After students have produced a few sentences using the new structure, erase the material from the chalkboard and continue the practice.

Conversation

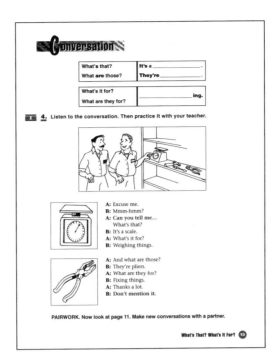

1. If there is a picture next to the conversation, have students look at it and talk about what's happening. Specific questions you may ask to get students to talk about the picture are provided in the *Teaching Suggestions* for each unit.

2. Some conversations are taped. If the unit has a taped conversation, play the tape.

3. Have students listen as you model the conversation line by line. To indicate when the speaker changes, use dolls or puppets, or turn your body from right to left.

4. Model the conversation a second time, and have students repeat it line by line.

5. Have two pairs of students stand up and model the conversation.

6. Tell students to close their books and look at the overhead transparency of the pictures on the first page of the unit. If you don't have an overhead projector, have students turn back to the first page of the unit.

7. Do the pairwork.

   a. First, model the task with one of the more capable students. Point to the first picture on the overhead transparency (or in your book). Ask the appropriate question and wait for the student to answer. Then switch roles: have the student ask you the question.

   b. Have two other students stand up and model the task again. Point to the second picture and have one of the students ask the appropriate question and the other student answer. Then have them switch roles.

   c. Finally, put students in pairs and have them begin the pairwork. Circulate to make sure they understand the task and to answer any questions.

Life Skill/Competency Listening Task

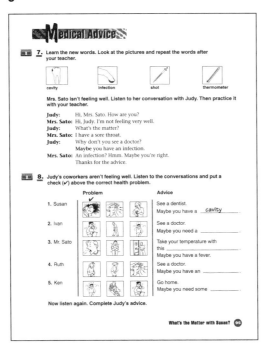

Many units contain listening activities that build students' aural comprehension in life skill and competency areas. The exact nature of these activities varies according to the life skill or competency focus, but all are task-based and have the same general format.

1. Prepare students for the listening task by introducing any new vocabulary items that appear at the top of the page. Direct students' attention to the captioned pictures and have them repeat the new vocabulary items after you. As you introduce each item, ask students yes/no and choice questions. For example, if the vocabulary item is *thermometer*, ask questions like these: *Joaquín, do you use a toothbrush or a thermometer to take your temperature?; Is there a thermometer in your kitchen/bedroom/bathroom?*

2. A dialogue introducing the life skill/competency focus follows the new vocabulary items. If this dialogue is taped, play the tape and then practice it with the class. If not, practice the dialogue with the class as follows.

   a. First, have students listen as you model the dialogue line by line. To indicate when the speaker changes, use dolls or puppets, or turn your body from right to left.

   b. Model the conversation a second time, and have students repeat it line by line.

   c. Practice the dialogue again by assuming the role of the first speaker and having the class take the role of the second speaker. Then switch roles.

3. Play the tape and have students listen to the instructions for the task. Then stop the tape and check to see that students have understood by asking them to state in their own words what they're going to do. Whatever the task may be, as students restate the instructions, reinforce them by drawing a circle, a check mark, or a line, or by filling in a blank, on the chalkboard.

4. Continue playing the tape until the end of the exercise. If students are instructed to listen again or if the task is difficult for your class, play the tape a second time.

5. Check students' answers by writing them on the chalkboard as students read them aloud or by having students write them on the chalkboard.

Information Gap

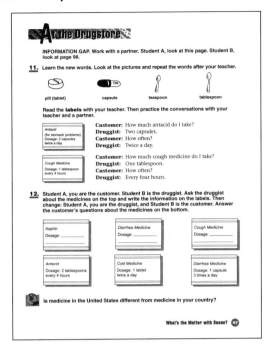 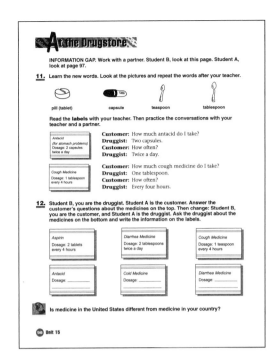

Units 3 and 15 include Information Gap activities.

1. Put students in pairs and designate one as Student A and the other as Student B. Check to see that students know which role they're playing by asking the A's, and then the B's, to raise their hands. Tell the A's to turn to the first page of the Information Gap exercise and the B's to turn to the second page. Have the A's, and then the B's, hold up their books to show they're on the right page.

2. Model any vocabulary items presented at the top of the page and have students repeat them. Then model the short conversations that follow and have students practice them with their partners.

3. Model the Information Gap activity. Designate yourself as Student A and one of the more capable students as Student B, showing the class that the two of you are looking at different pages. Ask Student B for the first piece of information missing on your page, and write down the answer in your book. Hold up your book to show the class the line you've drawn or the information you've written down. Then answer Student B's request for information. If you feel additional guidance is necessary, have two other students model the task again.

4. As students begin to work through the activity with their partners, circulate to make sure they've understood the instructions. There should be no flipping back and forth of pages if students are doing the activity correctly.

5. When students have finished the activity, check their answers by asking the A's and B's for the information missing from their respective pages and writing it on the chalkboard.

6. For more specific instructions as to how to present Information Gap activities, refer to the Teaching Suggestions for the two units in which they appear.

Culture Question

Each unit contains a culture question. These culture questions heighten students' cross-cultural awareness and provide a means for further exploration of the topic or life skill focus of the unit. All or some of the steps in the following procedure may be used to stimulate class discussion of the culture question.

1. Have one of the more capable students read the question aloud. For example: *Do most people in your country rent, or do they have their own homes?* As he or she reads, write the topic (housing) on the chalkboard.

2. Under the topic, make a complete list of students' native countries.

3. Have two or three students from each country (or region) answer the culture question. Write the answers beside the appropriate country.

4. Then ask a series of related questions. Yes/no and choice questions are easier to respond to than *Wh-* questions, but all types of questions may be appropriate depending on the abilities of individual students. For example, if a student says that most people have their own homes (in response to the question above), you may follow up with questions like these.

   Are the homes bigger or smaller than American homes?; How many bedrooms do houses generally have?; Do most newly married couples buy new homes or live in their parents' homes?

   If a student says that most people rent apartments, you may follow up with questions like these.

   Are apartments more expensive in your country or in the United States?; Do people who rent have to sign a lease?; Who pays the utilities?

5. As the course progresses, students will become more capable of working in small groups. If the culture question lends itself to small group work, for example, *What do people do in their leisure time in your country?* you may have students interact with their classmates in the following ways.

   a. Have students work with three or four classmates from the same country. In response to the culture question about leisure activities, have each group come up with a list of activities that are popular in their country. After the lists have been made, have group members put their lists on the chalkboard or share their information with the rest of the class.

   b. Have students work with three or four classmates from different countries. Ask group members to discuss the culture question among themselves, sharing information about which leisure activities are popular in their countries.

BEFORE UNIT 1
English for the Classroom

Topic: the classroom

Life Skills/Competencies: following directions; asking questions in class

Structure: imperatives

Vocabulary

Ask the question.	Study.	syllable
Answer.	Review.	singular
Write the words.	What does this mean?	plural
Write the sentence.	How do you pronounce this?	letters
Repeat.	What is the opposite?	alphabet
Continue.	How do you spell this?	vowels
Correct the mistake.	Give examples.	consonants

Teaching Suggestions

Activity 1

This unit is atypical in that the pictures on page 1 (and page 3) are captioned. Present each picture by simply modeling the target sentence and having students repeat.

Activity 2

After students have completed the matching exercise, use the following procedure to practice the sentences and check students' comprehension.

1. Write the following cues on the chalkboard: *name, day, time, age.* As you point to the individual cues, say *Ask the question* or *Answer the question.* For example:

   T: (pointing to *name*) Ask the question.

   S: What's your name?

   T: (pointing to *name*) Answer the question.

   S: My name is _____.

   Do not correct for accuracy. The point of the practice is appropriateness of response.

2. Say one of the following three cues: *1, 2 , 3; A, B, C; Monday, Tuesday, Wednesday.* Then follow the cue with one of these commands: *Repeat, Continue, Go on, Next.* For example:

   T: One, two, three...Repeat.

   S: One, two, three.

   T: One, two, three...Continue.

   S: Four, five, six...

3. Write the following sentences on the chalkboard. (Sentences 3 and 4 contain errors.)

   Please look at your book.

   Write your name on your paper.

   They is my friends.

   I name is Maria.

Point to individual sentences or words on the chalkboard as you say the commands and ask these questions.

Say the   word.   sentence.

How many words? sentences?

What's the first   word? sentence?

What's the last   word? sentence?

Correct the mistake.

For example:

      T: (pointing to *Please look at your book.*) What's the first word?

      S: Please.

      T: (pointing to *They is my friends.*) Correct the mistake.

      S: They are my friends.

4. Go back and practice the commands and questions again in random order.

Activity 4

After students have completed the matching exercise, use the following procedure to practice the questions and check students' comprehension.

Write the following words on the chalkboard: *big, little, unhappy, begin, fast, book, boys.*
Point to individual words on the chalkboard as you ask these questions.

What does this mean? (What's the meaning?); How do you pronounce this? (What's the pronunciation?); What's the opposite?; How do you spell this? (What's the spelling?); Give an example; How many syllables? vowels? consonants?; What's the first vowel? consonant?; Singular or plural?

For example:

      T: (pointing to *big*) What does this mean?

      S: Large.

      T: (pointing to *little*) How do you pronounce this?

      S: Little.

      T: (pointing to *unhappy*) What's the opposite?

      S: Happy.

      T: (pointing to *begin*) How do you spell this?

      S: B-e-g-i-n.

      T: (pointing to *fast*) Give an example.

      S: Airplane.

      T: (pointing to *little*) How many syllables?

      S: Two.

      T: (pointing to *begin*) How many consonants?

      S: Three.

      T: (pointing to *book*) Singular or plural?

      S: Singular.

UNIT 1 EXERCISES

A. Write the missing words. Use each word in the box once.

examples	mean	mistake
opposite	pronounce	question
sentence	spell	words

1. Ask the _____.

2. What is the _____?

3. Write the _____.

4. What does this _____?

5. How do you _____ this?

6. Give _____.

7. Correct the _____.

8. How do you _____ this?

9. Write the _____.

B. Read each answer. Then circle the letter of the correct question or sentence.

1. (a.) Ask the question.   What street do you live on?

   b. Answer the question.

2. a. What does this mean?   F-a-s-t.

   b. How do you spell this?

3. a. What does this mean?   Little. ➡ Small.

   b. What is the opposite?

4. a. Give examples.   Penny, nickel, dime.

   b. Correct the mistake.

5. a. How do you pronounce this?   Big. ➡ Little.

   b. What is the opposite?

6.   a.   Ask the question.   It's 4:00.

       b.   Answer the question.

7.   a.   What is the opposite?   I speak China. ➡ I speak Chinese.

       b.   Correct the mistake.

8.   a.   Write the sentence.   My telephone number is 555-1296.

       b.   Write the words.

Introductions

The main characters that appear throughout the Student Book are introduced on pages 5 and 6.

Page 5

Direct students' attention to the picture as you read the information at the bottom of the page. Then introduce the four characters by name, pointing to each one and asking these questions.

> *Where is he/she?; What is he/she doing?*

Then point to the characters and have students name them. Finally, ask these questions to check for comprehension.

> *Who's the boss?; Who's the new employee?; Are Ken and Judy married?*

Page 6

Direct students' attention to the picture as you read the information at the bottom of the page. Then point to Susan and ask these questions.

> *Who is this?; Where is she?; How many people are in Susan's family?; Where is Susan's husband?* (Students point to respond.); *What's his name?; What are Susan and Carlos doing?; How many children do Carlos and Susan have?; What are their names?; Where is Linda/Paul?* (Students point to respond.); *What is Linda/Paul doing?; How many pets does Susan's family have?; Do they have a dog?; Do they have a cat?; What's the cat doing?; Where is the parrot?* (Students point to respond.)

Review by pointing to the characters and having students name them.

What's Your Name?

Topic: personal information

Life Skill/Competency: introductions

Structure: formulaic questions

Vocabulary
What's your name?	Are you married? Do you have children?
Where are you from?	What do you do?
Where do you live?	What do you do on weekends?

Teaching Suggestions
Activity 1

Refer to the procedure on page v.

This unit is designed to provide: 1) a review of formulaic personal questions that ESL students generally study at the literacy level, and 2) a vehicle for you and your students to get to know each other. Look at page 8 while presenting the pictures on page 7. Ask each question of several students. The following is a sample presentation of Pictures 1 and 2 (*name* and *country*).

> Today we're going to talk about ourselves so we can get to know each other. What's your name? (pointing to Picture 1)...It's Tran. Is that your first name or your last name?...Your first name. And your last name?...Nham. Tran Nham. It's nice to have you in class. Where are you from, Tran? (pointing to Picture 2)...You're from Vietnam. What city are you from?...Oh, a little village by the beach. Nobody knows it. What's the name of your village?...You're right. I haven't heard of it. People say that the beach in Vietnam is very beautiful...It is? How many years did you live in Vietnam?...Twenty. I see. Now, how about you? What's your name?...

As you review these formulaic personal questions with the class, review personal pronouns and the present tense of *to be*, which students should already have mastered, by asking the class to repeat several students' answers. For example:

T:	What's your name?
F:	My name is Fungting Chan.
T:	What's her name, class?
Ss:	Her name is Fungting Chan.

T:	Where are you from, Juan?
J:	I'm from Mexico.
T:	And where are you from, Natalia?
N:	I'm from Mexico.
T:	Where are they from, class?
Ss:	They're from Mexico.

When repeating information given by their classmates in response to questions 3, 4, and 6, students may not use the correct verb forms. For example, they may give answers such as *He live in Richmond*. Do not correct for grammatical accuracy in these cases. Be concerned only with the content of students' responses.

Activity 2

Refer to the procedure on page vi.

Use this activity to introduce the concept of intonation. Write the six questions on the chalkboard. Model them one by one, asking students whether your voice goes up or down at the end of each question. Mark the intonation of the *Wh-* questions with falling arrows and the intonation of the yes/no questions with rising arrows.

What's your name? ↘   Are you married? ↗ Do you have children? ↗

Where are you from? ↘   What do you do? ↘

Where do you live? ↘   What do you do on weekends? ↘

Point out that falling intonation is used for *Wh-* questions and rising intonation is used for yes/no questions. Have students repeat the questions using the correct intonation. (To help students grasp the concept of rising and falling intonation, as you model the questions for them, make rising and falling gestures with your hand.) Then check students' understanding of question intonation by pointing to the questions one by one and having students interview you. Respond with information about yourself.

Activity 4

Refer to the procedure on page ix.

Before students start the pairwork, remind them to ask questions using the correct intonation.

After students finish the pairwork, ask them questions about their partners so they can share some of the information they have learned with the class.

Activities 5 and 6

Refer to the procedure on page x.

Point out that when we make third-party introductions, we use the word *this* to indicate people (*Judy,* this *is Susan Gomez.*) and not *he* or *she*.

Activity 7

After students listen to the conversation, point out that after exchanging names with a new acquaintance, we often inquire about that person's occupation before going on to ask other, more personal questions.

In addition, discuss the gestures that accompany introductions. Ask the class what gestures people make in their countries, and if those gestures depend on the sex and age of the people being introduced or the place where they meet. Explain that in the United States, when men are introduced or introduce themselves to each other, they often shake hands. A man and a woman may also shake hands, especially in a work-related context, but a handshake is rarely seen when two women are introduced except perhaps in business situations. Ask the class if they have seen other gestures being made during introductions, and explain when such gestures are appropriate.

Activity 8

Before students start interviewing their partners, ask two students to model the task. Remind students to use the correct intonation as they ask their questions.

Activity 9

Before students introduce their partners to the class, put the following cues on the chalkboard.

name

country

live

married/children

occupation

weekends

When students present their partners to the class, have them stand up and gesture toward their partners with an open hand.

For reinforcement of introductions, refer to Expansion Activities 1 and 2.

Expansion Activities

1. Put students in groups of three and have them write dialogues to practice third-party introductions. First, have students review the conversations on pages 9 and 10. Then instruct each group to write a conversation in which one student presents his or her friend to another student, and the two students being introduced inquire about each other's occupation and other personal information. When students have finished writing their dialogues, have them practice the dialogues aloud and then role-play them in front of the class. Encourage students to use hand gestures when they do their role-plays.

2. Dictate the following short paragraph for students to write.

    My name is Susan Gomez. I'm from the United States. I live in Los Angeles now. I'm married, and I have two children. I'm an office manager at the Ace Bicycle Factory. On the weekends, I walk in the park.

    Check students' comprehension by having volunteers write these sentences on the chalkboard in paragraph form. Then have students write about themselves, using the paragraph as a model.

A. **Read about the Sato family and the Gomez family.**

The Sato family is different from the Gomez family in several ways. To begin with, Mr. and Mrs. Sato live by themselves in an apartment. It's a small apartment on Hill Street. The Satos don't need a lot of room because their children don't live with them anymore. Two of their children are married and have houses of their own. The other two children are away at college. The Satos don't have any pets.

Susan and Carlos Gomez, on the other hand, live in a house on 22nd Street. It has three bedrooms, one for Susan and Carlos, another for their daughter, Linda, and a third for their son, Paul. The Gomez family also has pets. The cat sleeps in the living room with the parrot, who talks a lot and sometimes keeps the cat awake!

The Satos own the Ace Bicycle Factory. Mr. Sato is the boss, and he works a lot. He's usually at the factory from 8:00 A.M. to 6:00 P.M. six days a week. Mrs. Sato works at home. On Sundays, she and her husband work in their garden.

Both Susan and Carlos work outside their home. Susan is the office manager at the Ace Bicycle Factory, and Carlos is a construction worker. They never work on weekends. On Saturdays and Sundays, they like to play with their kids at the park or at the beach.

B. **Read the information. Which family does it tell you about? Write it under** *The Satos* **or** *The Gomezes*.

They have four children.

They have pets.

Their home is always noisy.

They own a bicycle factory.

They go to the park on weekends.

They live in a house.

Their children live away from home.

They're sometimes lonely.

They have jobs outside the home.

One of them works on Saturdays.

The Satos

The Gomezes

_____   _____

_____   _____

_____   _____

_____   _____

_____   _____

What's That? What's It For?

Topic: useful objects

Life Skill/Competency: requesting help

Structures: *to be*; plurals

Vocabulary

broom—sweep the floor	gloves—protect your hands	screwdrivers—fix things
mops—clean the floor	rulers—measure things	pliers—fix things
pail—hold water	scale—weigh things	scissors—cut things
sponges—wash dishes	light bulbs—light the room	closet
detergent—wash dishes	wastebasket—throw things away	cabinet
towels—dry things		drawer
iron—press clothes	hammer—fix things	

Teaching Suggestions
Activity 1

Refer to the procedure on page v.

When you ask what the items on page 11 are used for, students' responses needn't be restricted to those listed on page 12. The captions on page 12 are for students' reference, but appropriate variations or expansions should be encouraged.

Ask questions like the following to present the pictures.

What's this (called)?

What's this (used) for? Do you have a _____ at home?

Where do you keep your _____?

What color is your _____?

Do you ever use a _____? At work or at home?

How big is a _____?

The following is a sample presentation of Picture 1 (broom).

Today we're going to talk about things we use at work or at home. What's this picture of?...Well, is it a pencil or a broom?...Yes, it's a broom. How many parts to a broom?...Yes, a broom has two parts [pointing]. How big is a broom? This big? This big? [indicating with hands]...Yes, about this big. Do you have a broom in your house, Dac?...You do? Where do you keep your broom?...In the kitchen. And what's a broom used for?...Yes, it's for sweeping the floor. Where's the floor, everybody?...That's right [pointing]. Do you sweep the floor at home, Dac?...Oh, what a good husband! Marco, what color is the broom in your house? You don't know? My goodness, I'd hate to see the floor in your house!...Oh, I see, your wife does the sweeping. Well, OK then....

Grammar Box (page 13 of the Student Book)

Refer to the procedure on page viii.

Point to several items in the classroom—a pen, a clock, chairs, an eraser, chalk, a watch, books, a piece of paper, a bag, and some dollar bills—and have students name them. Then engage the class in dialogues similar to the following, using objects that are both singular and plural. For example:

> T: (pointing to a pen) What's that?
>
> Ss: It's a pen.
>
> T: What's it for? (making a writing gesture in the air)
>
> Ss: Writing.

After students have answered questions about all of the items, point to each object or group of objects and have half of the class ask the questions and the other half respond. Then have students switch roles.

Activity 4

Refer to the procedure on page ix.

As you practice the conversation with the students, point out that we often use the phrase *Can you tell me...* when asking for information from strangers. Also, explain that *Don't mention it* means *You're welcome.*

For reinforcement of household objects and their uses, refer to Expansion Activities 1, 2, and 3.

Activity 5

After students have written the nouns in plural form, teach them when to use the long and short endings on plural nouns. First, say these pairs of nouns aloud, clapping out the syllables: *day/days, fork/forks, stamp/stamps, bus/buses, box/boxes, watch/watches.* Go through the pairs of nouns again, having students first clap out the syllables and then repeat the nouns after you. Then write *long sound* and *short sound* at the top of two columns on the chalkboard. Say both the singular and plural forms of the regular nouns at the bottom of page 14. Have students tell you whether both forms of the noun have the same number of syllables or whether the plural form has an extra syllable. Write each noun in the appropriate column. Then circle the noun endings that require an additional syllable—*ch, x, sh,* and *s.* Explain that when nouns end with the sounds /ch/, /j/, /s/, /sh/, /x/, and /z/, the plural form will have an additional syllable. Point to the nouns again and have students pronounce the plural forms.

Activities 6 and 7

Refer to the procedure on page x.

Prepare students for the activities on pages 15 and 16 by asking these questions.

> *What do you do when you can't find something at work?; Who do you ask for help—your boss or a coworker?; Do you always get the help you need?*

As you introduce the vocabulary items, ask students what types of things are kept in closets, cabinets, and drawers.

Activity 9

After students have completed the conversations and practiced them with their partners, have several pairs of students perform their dialogues for the class.

Expansion Activities

1. Bring in realia or pictures of the household objects introduced on page 11. (Draw simple sketches on the chalkboard if you can't bring in realia or pictures.) Show them to the class one by one, and have students name them.

    Next, hold up flashcards (which you have made before class) with the names of the objects and have students read the words. Go through the flashcards a second time. As you hold each one up, make a true/false statement about what's it's used for. If your statement is true, students should respond with *yes*. If the statement is false, students should respond with *no* and say what the object is used for. For example:

    T: (holding up the word *pail*) It's for fixing things.

    Ss: No.

    T: What's it for, then?

    Ss: Holding water.

2. Give each student a notecard with the name of one of the objects. Then have each student come to the front of the classroom and mime using that object. As individuals are miming their actions, engage the rest of the class in dialogues like the following.

    T: What's he/she using?

    Ss: A scale.

    T: What's a scale for?

    Ss: Weighing things.

3. To further review household objects and their uses, play a game called "Right Chair, Wrong Chair." Move two chairs under the chalkboard. Above the chair on the left, write *Wrong*. Above the chair on the right, write *Right*. Divide the class into two teams. (If there is a fairly equal number of men and women in the class, it's fun to pit them against each other.)

    Now demonstrate how to play the game. Make a true statement such as *Gloves are for protecting your hands*. Ask the class whether your statement is right or wrong. After students say *right*, rush to the chair on the right, sit down, and point to the label *Right*. Then stand up again and make a false statement, such as *Pliers are for pressing clothes*. Ask the class whether your statement is right or wrong. After students say *wrong*, rush to the chair on the left, sit down, and point to *Wrong*. Next, have two students (from different teams) model the task. With chalk, draw a line on the floor about five or six feet away from the chairs; students must stand behind this line until they hear a statement. Tell them to listen for whether your statement is right or wrong, and to sit down in the appropriate chair. Then make a true/false statement. The student who sits in the appropriate chair first wins a point for his or her team. (If the first student to sit down sits in the incorrect chair, the other team wins a point.)

    Call on two more students (from different teams) to start the game. Continue playing until all of the students on each team have had a chance to compete. Keep score on the chalkboard. The team with the most points wins the game.

A. Write the missing words.

1. A _____ is for weighing things.

2. Mops are for _____ the floor.

3. _____ are for drying things.

4. An _____ is for pressing clothes.

5. Sponges are for _____ the dishes.

6. A _____ is for fixing things.

7. _____ are for protecting your hands.

8. A pail is for _____ water.

9. _____ is for washing the dishes.

10. A wastebasket is for _____ things away.

11. A broom is for _____ the floor.

B. Read this note to Ivan. Where are the things he needs to clean the house? Write *closet*, *cabinet*, or *drawer* under each picture.

> Dear Ivan,
>   Here's what you'll need to clean the house. The gloves and the sponges are in the drawer. The broom is in the closet. The mop is there too. The detergent is in the cabinet, and so are the towels. And...what else? The pail. It's in the closet.

closet

_____

_____

_____

_____

_____

Where's the Pail?

Topic: shelf locations

Life Skill/Competency: giving instructions

Structures: *to be*; prepositions of location

Vocabulary		
to the right of	over	on the top shelf
to the left of	above	on the bottom shelf
next to	under	on the second shelf from the top
on the far right	below	on the second shelf from the bottom
on the far left	beneath	on the middle shelf
on top of	behind	in the middle of the shelf

Teaching Suggestions

Activity 1

Refer to the procedure on page v.

Before you start asking questions to introduce shelf locations, do a quick review of the household objects on page 17. Have students look at this page and identify all of the items on each shelf.

Look at page 18 while presenting page 17. Read each statement, pointing to the items in the picture and clarifying the highlighted expression from the text. Then ask about other items in the picture (and in the classroom) to elicit answers using the same expression.

The following is a sample presentation of Expression 1 (to the right/left of).

> Today we're going to talk about shelves. What are shelves? Are there any in this room?...Yes, [pointing] those are shelves. How many shelves are there?...Four shelves. And what are shelves used for?...Yes, for keeping things. What do we keep on those shelves?...Books. Any shelves in your house, Natalia?...Yes? Where are they?...In your kitchen. Are there shelves where any of you work? Raise your hands....I see lots of you have shelves at work. And sometimes we need to say where things are on shelves. Look at these shelves now; look at the sponges and the pail [pointing with both hands]. Is the pail over the sponges?...No, it's... [emphasizing each word] to the right of the sponges. How many words was that [showing four fingers]?...Yes, four words: to the right of. And where are the sponges, then?...Yes, to the left of the pail. Now, look at the calendar and map on our wall [pointing]. Where's the map?...To the right of the calendar. And the door and window over there. Where's the window?...To the left of the door.

Activity 2

Refer to the procedure on page vi.

After students finish the pairwork, review familiar prepositions of location (such as *in, on,* and *next to*) and give the class additional practice with the new prepositions. Arrange several familiar objects—for example, a book, a pen, a notebook, a bag, a ruler, gloves, a pair of scissors, a sponge, and a towel—on a table at the front of the classroom. Call on individual students to come to the front of the classroom and rearrange the objects according to your instructions. For example:

Paco, please put the pen on top of the notebook.

Mei Ling, please put the towel behind the gloves.

Barbara, please put the bag on the far right.

After you've given lots of instructions, have one of the more capable students remain at the front of the classroom. Call on various members of the class to give the student instructions for rearranging the objects on the table. Have him or her carry out the instructions.

Activities 5 and 6

Refer to the procedure on page x.

As students listen to the conversation, write it on the chalkboard. Explain that the expression *Got it* is an informal way of saying *I understand*. Then model the dialogue line by line, asking students whether your voice goes up or down at the end of each utterance. Mark the intonation with rising and falling arrows.

Ken?

Yes?

Please put this screwdriver in the cabinet.

Sure. On which shelf?

On the top shelf, on the far right.

Top shelf, far right. Got it.

Explain that we generally use rising intonation when we call out and when we respond to people. Practice the conversation with the students using the correct intonation.

Reinforce this intonation pattern by doing a simple TPR* activity in which you make requests of individual students and students respond by performing the actions you have requested. Ask students to open and close things in your classroom, move things, and write and erase words from the chalkboard. Make your requests as follows, helping students with intonation as they respond. For example:

T: Maribel?

M: Yes?

T: Please close the door.

M: Sure. (getting up from her seat and closing the door)

T: Thank you.

M: You're welcome.

---

* Total Physical Response is a language-learning approach developed by James Asher. It focuses on language acquisition through nonthreatening, physically demonstrated listening comprehension.

Activity 7

Information Gap. Refer to the procedure on page xi. Since this is the first Information Gap activity in the book, spend considerable time preparing students to perform the task successfully.

Activity 8

After students finish the writing task, have the A's and the B's write their sentences on the chalkboard.

For reinforcement of shelf locations, refer to the Expansion Activity.

Expansion Activity

Draw an empty cabinet with five shelves on the chalkboard and have students draw a similar cabinet. (Tell them to use an entire page for their cabinets, as they'll need space to draw things on the shelves.) Then instruct them to draw various household objects on the shelves, using the prepositions of location introduced in this unit. For example:

Draw a wastebasket on the middle shelf, on the far left.

Draw two sponges to the right of the wastebasket.

Draw an iron above the sponges on the second shelf from the top.

After students have drawn all of the household objects on the shelves according to your instructions, check their comprehension of the instructions. Ask about the location of each object and have students tell you where to draw it on the shelves on the chalkboard.

Where are things on the shelves? Read the list. Then draw the things in their correct location on the shelves.

detergent—top shelf, far left	ruler—second shelf, in the middle
gloves—second shelf from the bottom, far left	scale—bottom shelf, in the middle
hammer—on the far left of the middle shelf	scissors—on the far left of the second shelf
iron—second shelf from the bottom, far right	screwdriver—middle shelf, far right
light bulbs—second shelf, far right	sponges—top shelf, in the middle
pail—bottom shelf, far right	towels—on the far right of the top shelf
pliers—in the middle of the middle shelf	wastebasket—bottom shelf, far left

 UNIT 4

Where's Judy?
What's She Doing?

Topic: stores and merchandise

Life Skill/Competency: giving directions

Structure: present continuous

Vocabulary

department store—buy clothes
bakery—buy bread and cake
hardware store—buy tools
grocery store/supermarket—buy food
auto repair shop—get the car fixed
barber shop/beauty salon—get a haircut
bank—get cash
furniture store—buy furniture
toy store—buy toys

thrift shop/secondhand store—buy used things
drugstore/pharmacy—buy medicine
parking lot—park the car
shoe store
card shop
bookstore
candy shop

Teaching Suggestions

Activity 1

Refer to the procedure on page v.

When you ask what the people on page 23 are doing at the various businesses, students' responses needn't be restricted to those listed on page 24. The captions on page 24 are for students' reference, but appropriate variations or expansions should be encouraged.

Ask questions like the following to present the pictures.

What is this (place)?

Who's at the _____?

What's he/she doing at the _____?

Where do *you* _____?

How far is your _____ from your house?

Is there a _____ near school?

The following is a sample presentation of Picture 1 (department store).

> Today we're going to talk about businesses. Look at this picture. Where is Judy?...Well, where do you buy clothes?...Yes, at a department store. What are some department stores in town?...Yes, Macy's...And Woolworth's. Those are both department stores...That's right, Mei. You can also buy other things at department stores. Do you live near a department store, Tho?...You live near Woolworth's? What about you, Angela? Is there a department store near your house?...There isn't. Now, back to our picture. Who's at the department store?...Yes, Judy is. And what's she doing there?...Well, is she buying food?...No. She's buying clothes.

Activity 2

Refer to the procedure on page vi.

Introduce the concept of stress and rhythm in the pronunciation of these noun phrases. First, write the businesses on the chalkboard with dots above the stressed syllables. For example:

department store   hardware store   grocery store
auto repair shop   beauty salon   parking lot

Model each phrase for the students. Then clap the rhythm, clapping hard on the stressed syllables, and softly and quickly on the unstressed syllables. Have the students first clap the rhythm and then repeat the phrase. Then go through the phrases again, pointing to each one and having students first clap the rhythm and then say the phrase aloud. When you finish, erase the phrases from the chalkboard.

Grammar Box (page 25 of Student Book)

Refer to the procedure on page viii.

Remind students that *-ing* is used to express actions occurring at the moment of speaking. Also, review the spelling rules for adding *-ing* to verbs. Write these three verbs on the chalkboard—*wait, take,* and *stop*—and ask students how to spell the *-ing* forms. If students can't state the spelling rules themselves, explain that we add only *-ing* except: 1) if the verb ends in *-e,* in which case the *-e* is dropped, and 2) if the verb ends in one consonant preceded by one vowel, in which case the final consonant is doubled.

Put the following list of verbs on the board and ask students to write the *-ing* forms.

run	study	dance	sleep	cry
write	swim	sit	walk	drive
read	play	leave	shop	cook

Next, have students practice using these verbs in sentences. Pass out notecards with each of the verbs to individuals or pairs of students. Ask each student or pair of students to come to the front of the classroom and mime their actions. Ask the rest of the class *What is Milagros doing?* or *What are Sanh and Robert doing?* Have the class report the actions using the correct pronouns and verb forms.

Activity 4

Before students do the writing task, ask several of them where their family members are and what they're doing. After they finish writing, have them share pairs of sentences with the class.

Activities 5 and 6

Refer to the procedure on page x.

Before listening to the conversation, ask students if they know of any shopping centers in their communities. Ask what kinds of stores are in these shopping centers and list them on the chalkboard.

For reinforcement of stores and businesses, refer to Expansion Activities 1 and 2.

Activity 7

After students finish the pairwork, have them write complete sentences about the locations of the stores. For example: *Betsy's Beauty Salon is on the fifth floor.*

Expansion Activities

1. To review stores and businesses, hold up flashcards (which you have made before class) with the names of the businesses and have students read the words. Then go through the flashcards a second time. As you hold each one up, make a true/false statement about what a person can do at that place. For example:

   T: (holding up the word *bakery*) You can buy clothes here.

   Ss: No.

   T: What *can* you do, then?

   Ss: Buy bread and cake.

2. Read each of the following short conversations aloud and have students say in which store they would likely hear such a conversation. To indicate when the speaker changes, use dolls or puppets, or draw two stick figures on the chalkboard and point to them as you speak.

A: I'll take this box of chocolates, please.

B: All right. Anything else?

A: How short do you want your hair cut?

B: Cut an inch off the back and sides.

A: OK.

A: Can I park my car here?

B: Yes, sir. Parking is $5 an hour.

A: $5 an hour? That's crazy!

A: I'd like to cash this check.

B: All right. Sign your name on the back, please.

A: Hi. I'm looking for a hammer. Where can I find one?

B: Aisle 3.

A: Thank you.

A: Hey! This beautiful wool jacket is only $2.50!

B: Wow! And it looks so nice on you!

A: Do you sell ESL books?

B: Yes. They're on the second floor.

A: Are these bananas on sale?

B: Yes, they are. They're only 29¢ a pound.

A: Is this bread fresh?

B: Yes, ma'am. We bake bread every morning.

A: Let's stop here for a minute.

B: Why?

A: I need to buy my father a birthday card.

A: What year is your car?

B: It's a 1988.

A: And what's the problem?

B: It won't start.

A: I'm sorry, sir, but we don't have this medicine.

B: You don't? Then where can I get it?

A: Try Doc's Pharmacy down the street.

A. Read Judy's letter to her friend Debbie. Where are Judy and her coworkers? Look at the pictures of the locations and write the names of the people below.

Dear Debbie,   October 9

    I can't believe it! It's 1:00 on Wednesday afternoon, and I'm the only one here at work. So I can stop working and write this letter to you.

    Everyone's out this afternoon. Mr. Sato is at a furniture store. He's looking for a new desk for his office. Susan's kids are sick, so she's buying some medicine at the drugstore. Andy's car isn't working. He's getting it fixed at an auto repair shop. Ruth is taking money to the bank. Ivan and Ken aren't here either! They're buying new tools at a hardware store.

    So what am I doing here? Why am I here at this bicycle factory all alone? Uh-oh! Someone's coming in the door. I have to get back to work.

Love,
Judy

_____

_____

_____

_____

_____

_____

B. Write what the people are doing.

1. *Mr. Sato is looking for a desk at a furniture store.* _____

2. _____

3. _____

4. _____

5. _____

6. _____

 **Where's Susan Going?**

Topic: getting around town

Life Skill/Competency: giving street directions

Structures: present continuous; prepositions of motion

Vocabulary

across the street	around the corner	through the park
up the hill/ to the top of the hill	around the block	across the bridge
down the hill/ to the bottom of the hill	along the river	toward the window
down the street	through the window	away from the window

Teaching Suggestions
Activity 1

Refer to the procedure on page v.

During the presentation and conversation practice in this unit, students will be asked a question whose answer is not given in the book: *Why is this person going to this place?* Here, as in other places indicated in the book, the aim is to reinforce the new language—and have some fun— by engaging in free speculation.

For each picture, first ask the following two questions.

Where's this person going/walking?

Why is he/she going _____? (free speculation)

Then demonstrate or elicit other examples of the prepositions being taught, as in this sample presentation of Picture 1 (across the street).

> Today we're going to talk about people walking and driving places. First, let's look at Susan. Where's Susan going?…Is she walking across the room?…No. She's walking across the street. By the way, what do we always have to do before we walk across the street?…Yes, we need to wait for the green light. And look both ways. Now, why do you think Susan is going across the street? Any ideas?…Yes, maybe she sees her friend on the other side. Any other ideas why she's walking across the street?…Yes, maybe she's going to the store. Why else might she be going across the street?…

Activity 2

Refer to the procedure on page vi.

Work on stress and rhythm in the pronunciation of the prepositional phrases. First, write the phrases on the chalkboard with dots above the stressed syllables. For example:

ac·ross the street   up the hill   away from the window

Model each phrase for the students. Then clap the rhythm, clapping hard on the stressed syllables, and softly and quickly on the unstressed syllables. Have the students first clap the rhythm and then repeat the phrase.

Go through the phrases again, pointing to each one and having students first clap the rhythm and then say the phrase aloud. When you finish, erase the phrases from the chalkboard.

Before students start the pairwork, give them additional practice with the prepositional phrases. On the chalkboard, draw simple diagrams of: 1) a hill, 2) a park bordered on all sides by streets, 3) a bridge, and 4) a window. Begin by pointing to a spot at the base of the hill and saying *I'm walking, and I'm right here. Can I go up the hill?* After the class has responded in the affirmative, ask a student to come to the chalkboard and show you how to do it with a gesture of the hand. Draw a broken line to indicate the appropriate movement. Continue the practice with these questions.

> *Can I go down the hill?; Can I go across the hill?; Can I go through the hill?; Can I go around the hill?*

As the class responds to your questions, have individual students come to the chalkboard and draw the broken lines representing successive possible movements. When the answer to a question is *no,* e.g., I can't go *through* the hill on foot, corroborate the students' negative response with a shake of your head and a motion of your hand demonstrating the impossibility of this movement. Then use the diagram of the park surrounded by streets to talk about movement relating to the park, the street, the corner, and the block. Use the diagrams of the bridge and the window in a similar way. Then have students begin the pairwork.

Grammar Box (page 31 of Student Book)

Refer to the procedure on page viii.

Remind students that we use *is/are* + _____ing to talk about actions occurring at the moment of speaking. Hold up large pictures of people going places (on foot, on bicycles, on motorcycles, or in cars, buses, trains, or planes) and ask members of the class to speculate in response to your questions from the grammar box. For example:

> T: (holding up a picture of a woman walking toward a drugstore)
>
> Where's she going, Ramona?
>
> R: To the drugstore.
>
> T: Why is she going there?
>
> R: Because she's feeling sick and she needs medicine.

The point of this practice is to get students indulging in free speculation about where the people in the pictures are going and why they're going there. Go through the pictures a second time, and have the class ask the questions from the grammar box and individual students respond.

In addition, point out that we use *is/are* + _____ing to talk about actions in the future. Practice this by asking several students where they're going after class and tomorrow morning. For further information on the use of the present continuous to express actions in the future, refer to *Going Places* Student Book 1, Unit 8.

Activity 4

Refer to the procedure on page ix.

For reinforcement of prepositions of motion, refer to Expansion Activity 1.

Activity 6

Prepare students for this activity by drawing on the chalkboard a simple street map of the immediate area surrounding your school. Have students volunteer information about street names and the location of prominent landmarks such as buildings, businesses, hills, rivers, and bridges. Then choose a starting point and have students give you directions from that point to various other places on the map. As students give the directions, trace the route with your finger to demonstrate how to use the map to arrive at the desired locations.

After you've located several places on your map of the surrounding neighborhood, direct students' attention to the street map on page 32. Acquaint students with the features on the map by asking these questions.

> *What streets are on this map?; Is there a river on the map? Where is it?; How many bridges are there?; Is there a hill on the map? Where is it?*

Before listening to the conversations, read the names of the businesses with the students. Then hold up your book and point to the starting point.

After students finish the task, check to see that they've located the businesses correctly by asking them for directions to each of the businesses on the map.

For reinforcement of street directions, refer to Expansion Activity 2.

Expansion Activities

1. To review prepositions of motion, do the following TPR activity. First, call on individual students to respond to instructions like these.

    Van Thu, please stand up.

    Now walk toward the window.

    Now walk along the side of the room.

    Now walk toward your seat.

    Now sit down.

    Next, perform the actions yourself and have students say what you're doing. For example:

    > T: Class, what am I doing now?
    >
    > Ss: You're walking across the room.

2. For a challenging activity involving street directions, make photocopies of an enlarged segment of a street map of your city. Put students in groups of three or four and hand each group a map. First, help them locate some city landmarks noted on the map— prominent buildings/businesses, parks, hospitals, schools. Next, write on the chalkboard a list of places to go to and from. For example:

    town square ➡ Mercy Hospital

    school ➡ Norman Park

    federal building ➡ bus station

    downtown library ➡ May's Department Store

    Have students work with the other members of their group to write directions from one place to the other. Then have the different groups share their information with the class, encouraging students from other groups to listen carefully and trace the routes on their maps to check for accuracy.

A. Read about the stores near Carlos and Susan's house.

Carlos and Susan live **halfway** up a hill near lots of shops. The bakery is one block down the hill. The candy shop is across from the bakery. At the bottom of the hill is a bridge. The grocery store is across the bridge.

The hardware store is two blocks up the hill. The drugstore is around the corner from the hardware store. There's a park across from the drugstore. The card shop is on the other side of the park.

Carlos and Susan like living near so many shops. It's very **convenient.**

B. Carlos is going shopping this afternoon. Read his shopping list. Then number the sentences below in the correct order.

> 1. hammer
> 2. medicine
> 3. birthday card
> 4. chocolate candy
> 5. bread
> 6. milk and eggs

_____ Then he's going across the street.

_____ Then he's going through the park.

__1__ First, he's going up the hill.

_____ Next, he's going down the hill.

_____ Finally, he's going across the bridge.

_____ Next, he's going around the corner.

Now write where Carlos is going.

Carlos is going shopping this afternoon. First,

_____

_____

_____

_____

UNIT 6 Where Was Carlos during the Earthquake?

Topic: community resources

Life Skill/Competency: using the telephone

Structure: past of *to be*

Vocabulary   library—read a magazine
bus station—meet a friend
day-care center—take a nap
clinic—wait for the doctor
hospital—visit a friend
playground—play basketball

police station—talk about a problem
airport—leave on a trip
post office—buy stamps
employment office—ask about jobs
museum—look at pictures
church—sing

Teaching Suggestions
Activity 1

Refer to the procedure on page v.

The background for the presentation is an earthquake that happened "yesterday at 2:47 P.M." Ask where each of the people on page 33 was at the time of the quake and what he or she was doing. As in Unit 4, students may suggest other activities that the various people were doing at the different places, and this is to be encouraged.

Ask questions like the following to present the pictures.

What is this (place)?

What was this person doing at the _____?

What else can we do at a _____?

Is there a _____ near your house?

How often do you go to the _____?

Are there many _____ in our city?

The following is a sample presentation of Picture 1 (Carlos reading a magazine at the library).

> Well, class, I have some sad news. Yesterday, in Carlos's city, there was a big earthquake at 2:47 in the afternoon. Do you know what an earthquake is?...Yes, [indicating with hands and body] it's when buildings and houses shake. Do you like earthquakes?...No. They're scary, aren't they? Did any of you have an earthquake in your country?...Yes, Anita. The earthquake in Mexico City was very big....And you say there are always earthquakes in Japan, Yoshiko? I wouldn't like that! Now, let's look where everyone was during yesterday's earthquake. Where was Carlos?...This is a building with lots of books....Yes, it's a library. Carlos was at the library. Is there a library near school?...Yes, there's a library on Stockton Street. And is there a library near your house?...There's a library near your house, Ulises? Do you ever go to the library?...You do. Now, what do you think Carlos was doing at the library yesterday?...Yes, maybe he was reading a book. Or, do you know what a magazine is?...Yes, a magazine comes out every week, or every month. Does anyone have a magazine with them now?...Show it to the class, Ana. What's your magazine about?...Oh, it's a magazine about movie stars! Anyone else read magazines?...

Activity 4

Prepare students for the listening activity by asking the following questions.

What time does our school open? What time does it close?; Is there a post office near your house?

What time does it open/close?; Is there a library near your house? What time does it open/close?

Grammar Box (page 35 of Student Book)

Refer to the procedure on page viii.

Have students practice the new structures. First, hand six individuals and pairs of students notecards (which you have made before class) bearing these commands.

Go to the chalkboard. Write your name.

Go to the calendar. Point to the date today.

Go to my desk. Open my book and read.

Go to the map. Point to your country.

Go to the window. Look outside.

Go to the front of the room. Say the alphabet.

Have the student with the first notecard get up from his or her seat, follow the instructions, and sit down again. Then have the class respond to your questions with short answers. For example:

T:	Where was she?
Ss:	At the chalkboard.
T:	What was she doing?
Ss:	Writing her name.

Continue the practice by having other individuals and pairs of students with notecards carry out their instructions and the class report their actions. After the class has reported the actions of two or three students, supply cues so that the class will ask the questions and individuals will respond. For example:

T:	Where.
Ss:	Where were they?
T:	Mai.
M:	At the window.
T:	What.
Ss:	What were they doing?
T:	Roberto.
R:	Looking outside.

Activity 5

Refer to the procedure on page ix.

For reinforcement of community resources, refer to Expansion Activities 1 and 2.

Grammar Box (page 36 of Student Book, top)

Refer to the procedure on page viii.

Put the following list of past time expressions on the chalkboard.

at 7:00 last night	last summer
at 10:00 yesterday morning	two years ago
last Sunday afternoon	five years ago

Using these time expressions, ask students questions from the grammar box and have them respond with short answers. Then point to the time expressions one by one and have students ask you questions. Respond with short answers.

Grammar Box (page 36 of Student Book, middle)

Refer to the procedure on page viii.

Cue students and have them produce sentences about their activities and the activities of their friends and family yesterday. For example:

> T: At 11:00 A.M., your husband, Suhua.
>
> S: At 11:00 A.M., my husband was making bread at work.
>
> T: At 4:00 P.M., your children, Vinh.
>
> V: At 4:00 P.M., my children were doing their homework at home.

Activity 7

After students finish the writing task, have them share some of their sentences with the class.

Activity 8

After students have alphabetized the libraries, help them with the pronunciation of the street addresses and telephone numbers. First, put these addresses on the chalkboard with slash marks.

54 1st St.	1/0/8 1st St.	2/16 1st St.
11/0/7 1st St.	22/39 1st St.	1/1/8/9/6 1st St.

Have students repeat these addresses after you. Then have them read the addresses of the branch libraries. Help them with the pronunciation of the numbers.

Then put the following telephone numbers on the chalkboard with slash marks indicating a pause between the third and fourth digits.

982/-/9573   367/-/4870   583/-/5072

Explain that when we say a telephone number, we generally pause between the third and fourth digits. Model the numbers and have students repeat them after you. Then have students read the rest of the telephone numbers from the directory.

As you practice the conversation with the students and students make new conversations with their partners, help them with the pronunciation and intonation of the addresses and telephone numbers.

Activities 10, 11, and 12

Refer to the procedure on page x.

If a map of the United States is available, have students point to the four cities on the map. Ask if they have visited these cities and, if so, what they're like.

Prepare students for the directory-assistance activities by asking these questions.

> What do you do if you want to call someone but you don't know their telephone number?
>
> What number do you call for a local number?
>
> What number do you call for a long-distance number?
>
> Who do you talk to?

As students practice the conversations with their partners, remind them to use the correct intonation when giving phone numbers.

For more practice calling directory assistance, refer to Expansion Activity 3.

Expansion Activities

1. To review community resources, hold up flashcards (which you have made before class) with the names of the resources and have students read the words. Go through the flashcards a second time. As you hold each one up, make a true/false statement about what people do there. If your statement is true, students should respond with *yes*. If the statement is false, students should respond with *no*. Then call on a student to correct your statement. For example:

   T: (holding up the word *library*) You can sing here.

   Ss: No.

   T: What *can* you do here, Mai?

   M: Read a book.

2. Read each of the following short conversations aloud and have students say in which place they would likely hear such a conversation. To indicate when the speaker changes, use dolls or puppets, or draw two stick figures on the chalkboard and point to them as you speak.

   A: Can I have ten 50-cent stamps, please?

   B: Sure. That's $5.00.

   A: Where are the magazines?

   B: They're on the second floor, to the left.

   A: Is the 4:15 bus from Seattle here yet?

   B: I'm sorry, sir. That bus is late.

   A: When's the next plane to Hong Kong?

   B: It leaves in two hours. Do you want to buy a ticket?

   A: I have an appointment with Dr. Blackman at 3:30.

   B: Please have a seat, ma'am. The doctor will be with you in a few minutes.

   A: I'm a construction worker, and I need a job.

   B: OK. Please fill out these forms.

   A: Where's Tim?

   B: He's over there playing soccer.

   A: Do you have pictures from Korea?

   B: Yes, we do. They're on the third floor.

   A: My friend is sick. His name is Minh Ho.

   B: Minh Ho? Yes. Mr. Ho is in Room 208.

   A: Where's my son?

   B: He's over in the corner playing with the toy cars.

3. For homework, give students a list of six to eight community resources and businesses in your area. Have them find the telephone numbers (and addresses) of these establishments by using the telephone directory and/or calling directory assistance.

Look at this page from the telephone directory. Write answers to the questions below.

Health Clinics

Internal Medicine Clinic	707 Fairview at Pine........	774-0905
International Medical Group	1114 Stone St...................	648-5572
Life and Health Clinic	68 East Lake Dr..............	982-6701
Lifeline Health Center	13098 Boyer Ave.............	466-7812
Medical Advice Clinic	192 44th Ave...................	568-4530
Medical Service Center	2486 Golden Dr................	(204) 246-2385
Medicine for Women	355 Mill St.......................	367-9793
National Children's Clinic	1110 Stone St...................	648-6002
National Health Network	49 Market St....................	466-8400
Neo-Natal Health Care	10028 River at Hill...........	774-3886
North Shore Clinic	677 Crest Dr....................	568-5670
Ocean Medical Group	741 88th Ave...................	(204) 246-1874

1. What's the telephone number of the Medical Advice Clinic? _____

2. What's the telephone number of the Medical Service Center? _____

3. Are the Medical Advice Clinic and the Medical Service Center in the

    same city? _____ How do you know? _____

4. What's the address of Lifeline Health Center? _____

5. What corner is the Internal Medicine Clinic on? _____

6. What other clinic is on the same street as the National Children's

    Clinic? _____

7. Is Neo-Natal Health Care in the middle of the block? _____

8. What's the telephone number of Ocean Medical Group? _____

9. What street is the Life and Health Clinic on? _____

10. What's the name of the health clinic for women? _____

11. What's the telephone number of the clinic for children? _____

12. What's the name of the clinic on Crest Drive? _____

 **UNIT 7**

Is There a Listening Lab at Our School?

Topic: school facilities

Life Skill/Competency: inquiring about classes

Structure: *there is/there are*

Vocabulary   listening lab   computers   copy machine   vending machines
typing classes   counselors' office   night classes   bookstore
library   tape recorders   student lounge   emergency exit

Teaching Suggestions
Activity 1

Refer to the procedure on page v.

Ask questions like the following to present the pictures.

What do people do at a _____? *or* What's a _____ for?

Is there/Are there _____ at our school?

Where is/are the _____ at our school?

Where else can we find _____?

Do you ever use the _____ at our school?

The following is a sample presentation of Picture 1 (listening lab).

> Today we're going to talk about things we find in schools. Do you know what this is?…Yes, it's a listening lab. What do people do at a listening lab?…Yes, students listen to tapes. Is there a listening lab at our school?…Yes, there is. Where is our listening lab?…It's across the hall, in Room 209. Does anybody ever use the listening lab here?…You do, Alex? What do you use the listening lab for?…For listening to the tape of our book. Does anyone else use the listening lab?…You do, Salvador? When do you use it?…

Grammar Box (page 41 of Student Book)

Refer to the procedure on page viii.

Write the following questions and answers on the chalkboard. As you model them, ask students whether your voice goes up or down at the end of the questions and how your voice changes in pitch as you say the answers. Mark the intonation pattern for yes/no questions and short answers with arrows.

T: Is there a baby in the classroom?

Ss: No, there isn't.

T: Are there any lights in the classroom?

Ss: Yes, there are.

Have students repeat the questions and answers with the correct intonation. Then write on the chalkboard a list of singular and plural objects that might or might not be found in the classroom. Point to the words on the list one at a time and have half of the students ask questions and the other half respond. For example:

T: (pointing to the word *desk*)

Ss1: Is there a desk in the classroom?

Ss2: Yes, there is.

T: (pointing to the word *cabinets*)

Ss1: Are there any cabinets in the classroom?

Ss2: No, there aren't.

Help students produce sentences with the correct intonation.

Activity 4

Refer to the procedure on page ix.

If students are not yet familiar with their school and its facilities, after you practice the conversations together, take the class on a quick tour of the building, stopping to note the different types of classrooms and facilities and the location of the offices, machines, and exits. Then return to your classroom and have students begin the pairwork.

For reinforcement of questions with *Is there/Are there,* refer to Expansion Activity 1.

Activity 6

Prepare students for this activity by reviewing the stores and businesses introduced in Unit 4. Put a transparency of the pictures on page 23 on the overhead projector (or ask students to turn to page 23 in their books). Point to the pictures in random order and have students say the names of the businesses and what you can do there.

After you practice the conversations with the students, write on the chalkboard the responses to the question *How far?* from the box. Model the pairwork by asking several students about businesses in their neighborhoods.

Grammar Box (page 43 of Student Book)

Refer to the procedure on page viii.

Have students turn to the chart they filled in on page 41 and make sentences about their school using *There is* and *There are.* Start by making the first sentence yourself. For example, *There are two restrooms on the first floor and two restrooms on the second floor.* Then have students make sentences about the other facilities and machines listed in the chart.

Activity 7

Before students start the writing task, supply them with verbal cues and have them make sentences aloud about their neighborhoods. For example:

T: Playground, Juan.

J: There aren't any playgrounds in my neighborhood.

After students finish writing, have them share some of their sentences with the class.

For reinforcement of statements with *There is/There are,* refer to Expansion Activity 2.

Activity 8

Refer to the procedure on page x.

After students listen to the messages, ask them if they have ever heard recorded messages on the telephone. If so, ask who they were calling, what they wanted to find out, and if they understood the message.

Activity 9

As you go over the names of the classes with the students, explain the meaning of unfamiliar words. Ask students what you learn in the different classes and if they or anyone in their family has taken these types of classes.

Activity 10

Students may not know all the different types of classes offered at their school. As they make conversations with their partners, circulate and answer any questions that arise.

Expansion Activities

1. Review questions and answers with *Is there/Are there* with a mingling activity in which students move around the room asking their classmates questions. Pass out copies of (or have students copy from the chalkboard) the following form.

Find 3 people with a thrift shop in their neighborhood. 1. _____ 2. _____ 3. _____	Find 3 people with a church in their neighborhood. 1. _____ 2. _____ 3. _____
Find 3 people with a museum in their neighborhood. 1. _____ 2. _____ 3. _____	Find 3 people with a bakery in their neighborhood. 1. _____ 2. _____ 3. _____

Before starting the activity, read the instructions with the students and model the task. Circulate and ask several students if there's a thrift shop in their neighborhood. Write the names of those who answer in the affirmative on your form. Help students recall the correct intonation for yes/no questions (rising) and short answers (rising/falling) and remind them to use the correct intonation patterns as they ask and answer questions. Then have all students stand up and begin interviewing their classmates.

2. Review the vocabulary for tools and common household objects and give students additional practice formulating sentences with *There is/There are*. Write this list of cues on the chalkboard.

mops—top shelf

wastebasket—bottom shelf

sponges—middle shelf

hammers—second shelf from the top

detergent—middle shelf

brooms—top shelf

pail—bottom shelf

scissors—second shelf from the bottom

pliers—top shelf

light bulbs—second shelf from the top

Have students turn to page 17 and, using the above cues, write sentences about the objects on the shelves. Help them get started by asking if there are any mops on the top shelf. When students answer *no*, write this sentence on the chalkboard: *There aren't any mops on the top shelf.* When students finish the writing task, collect their papers.

A. **Read about the branch campuses at Cowen Community College.**

- The **North Shore Branch** is located at 3442 3rd Avenue. It offers classes in the morning and afternoon. There are classes in science, mathematics, social science, English, and foreign language. There's a library in the middle of the campus. There's a student parking lot on the corner of 3rd and Elm.

- The **East Shore Branch** is located at 21000 Lakeland Drive. It offers classes in the morning and afternoon. There are classes in business, typing, and computer science. There are computers in every classroom. There's a bookstore on the west side of the campus. There is no student parking lot.

- The **South Shore Branch** is located at 847 Homer Street. It offers classes in the morning and at night. There are classes in ESL, citizenship, and driver's education. There's a listening lab in Building E. Students can park their cars on Homer Street.

B. **Look at the pictures and write sentences with *There is* and *There are*.**

1. There's a library at the North Shore Branch.

2. _____

3. _____

4. _____

5. _____

UNIT 8 | How Many Rooms Are There in the Apartment?

Topic: housing

Life Skill/Competency: looking for housing

Structures: *there is/there are* (count and non-count nouns)

Vocabulary

How many rooms are there in the apartment?

Is the apartment furnished or unfurnished?

Is there parking?

Is there a washer and dryer?

What's the location of the apartment?

How much is the rent?

Who pays utilities?

How much is the deposit?

How long is the lease for?

| closets | cabinets | stores | traffic | crime |
| windows | trees | furniture | noise | light |

Teaching Suggestions

Activity 1

Refer to the procedure on page v.

Introduce this unit by telling students they will be practicing questions people ask when looking for an apartment. Look at page 46 as you present page 45, asking the question that is given beside each picture. Ask students the questions about their own apartments, reinforcing the target vocabulary by having them elaborate on their answers, and then ask if they can make the questions. During the presentation, and again before beginning the pairwork in Activity 3, have volunteers model the questions as the students look at the pictures.

After you introduce the question *Who pays utilities?* in item 7, point to the individual utilities in the picture (or draw rough sketches on the chalkboard) as you ask students these questions: *Who pays for gas/electricity/water/garbage collection in your apartment?*

The following is a sample presentation of Picture 1 (How many rooms are there in the apartment?).

> Today we're going to talk about the questions we need to ask when we look for an apartment. First, we ask [pointing to the first picture] how many...yes; how many rooms in the apartment. Ruben, how many rooms are in your apartment?...Four rooms? What are they?...I see. And you, Huang? How many rooms are there in your apartment?...Two rooms. You live alone. Now, can you make the question? "How many...?" You want to try, Pedro?...Very good. Anyone else want to try?...

Activity 2

Use this activity to contrast the intonation of yes/no and *Wh-* questions. Before you begin, write the nine questions on the chalkboard. Model them one by one, asking students whether your voice goes up or down at the end of each question. Mark the intonation of the *Wh-* questions with falling arrows and the intonation of the yes/no questions with rising arrows.

How many rooms are there in the apartment?↘

Is the apartment furnished?↗

Ask students why questions 2, 3, and 4 have rising intonation and the others have falling intonation. Help them recall that yes/no questions generally have rising intonation and *Wh-* questions generally have falling intonation. Have students repeat the questions with the correct intonation. Help them by making rising and falling gestures with your hand. Then check students' understanding of the intonation patterns by pointing to the questions one by one and having students interview you about your apartment or house.

Then have students do the pairwork. Remind them to ask questions with the correct intonation.

Activity 3

Refer to the procedure on page ix.

Have students look at the For Rent sign and ask where they've noticed such signs in their neighborhoods.

After students listen to the conversation, engage them in a discussion about landlords and managers. Ask several apartment dwellers these questions.

> *Do you know your landlord? What's his/her name?; Does he/she live in your apartment building?;*
>
> *Is there a manager for your building? What's his/her name?; Does he/she live in the building?;*
>
> *Who do you write the rent check to?; Who do you talk to about problems in your apartment?*

Explain that while landlords are the owners of apartment buildings, they don't always live in the buildings they own. Managers, on the other hand, generally live in the buildings they care for and often have the task of renting vacant apartments.

For more practice with questions about housing, refer to Expansion Activity 1.

Activity 4

Prepare students for this activity by writing the abbreviations of a few days and months on the chalkboard. Ask students to come to the board and write the words these abbreviations stand for. Then ask if students know of any other abbreviations, and write them on the chalkboard too.

Circulate as students work through this activity, urging them to skip items they don't know. After they've written out as many of the abbreviations as they can with their partners, have volunteers write them on the chalkboard. Spell out the words for any abbreviations students are unfamiliar with, and then go through and clarify the meanings of all the abbreviations.

Activity 5

After students have finished writing answers to the questions, check their work by asking for volunteers to write the answers on the chalkboard.

For more practice with For Rent ads, refer to Expansion Activity 2.

Activity 6

Look at page 49 (or an overhead transparency of the page) while presenting the pictures.

For each of pictures 1–5, ask students *Are there many _____ in your house /neighborhood?* (There is no new vocabulary represented by these pictures.)

The vocabulary represented by pictures 6–10 (except for *furniture*) has not yet appeared in the book, so first clarify the meaning of each word. Then ask students *Is there much _____ in your house/neighborhood?*

Grammar Box (page 49 of Student Book)

Refer to the procedure on page viii.

Explain that *are* and *many* are used in questions with count nouns and *is* and *much* are used in questions with non-count nouns. Then practice the material as follows. First, put two lists on the chalkboard, one of count nouns in the classroom and the other of non-count nouns.

count nouns	*non-count nouns*
students	light
teachers	noise
windows	furniture
cabinets	chalk

Then have students respond to your questions. For example:

> T: Are there many students in the classroom?
>
> Ss: Yes, there are.

Then point to the nouns one by one and have students ask you the questions.

Grammar Box (page 50 of Student Book, top)

Have students ask you questions about your home and neighborhood using the pictures in Activity 8.

Grammar Box (page 50 of Student Book, middle)

Point out that while *much* is used only with non-count nouns and *many* is used only with count nouns, *a lot of* and *any* are used with both count and non-count nouns.

Activity 9

After you read the examples with the students, supply cues and have several students produce sentences orally before they start the writing task. For example:

> T: Crime, Angeles.
>
> A: There isn't much crime in my neighborhood.

After students finish writing, have them share some of their sentences with the class. For reinforcement of count and non-count nouns, refer to Expansion Activity 3.

Expansion Activities

1. Strip Story. Using the dialogue on page 47 of the Student Book as a model, type out a new dialogue that includes some of the questions from page 46 and cut it into strips of paper, with one strip per line of text. Put students into pairs and give each pair all of the strips necessary to create the dialogue. (The strips should not be in order.) Ask students to arrange the strips to create a conversation. Then have them practice the conversation aloud.

2. Photocopy some For Rent ads from your local newspaper. Pass these out to the students and have them rewrite the ads with their partners, spelling out the abbreviated words. Then ask them questions about the apartments. For example:

   How many bedrooms are there in the first apartment?

   Who pays utilities?

   Is the second apartment furnished or unfurnished?

   Who can you call about it?

Finally, have students choose an apartment they're interested in and, with a partner, write out a list of questions they would want to ask the manager or landlord on the telephone.

3. Call students' attention to the additional non-count nouns listed at the bottom of page 50. Put these cues on the chalkboard.

There is—fog, rain, snow, wind

eat—meat, rice, sugar

drink—coffee, milk, tea, water

have—money, work, time

Then write the following example sentences next to the cues.

There's a lot of fog in San Francisco.

There isn't any snow in San Francisco.

I eat a lot of rice.

I don't drink much milk.

I don't have any money.

Ask students to write fourteen sentences about their cities and themselves. When students finish the writing task, collect their papers.

A. Read the information in the For Rent ads. Then write answers to the questions below.

Ocean view apartment!	Convenient downtown location!	Near Englewood Park!
• 3 BR, 2 bath • pkg. garage • $1200/mo. • W/D, new cpt. Myers Realty, 362-1108	• 2 BR apt. • avail. 6/1 • $1000/mo., util. incl. • nr. bus James Lowe, 857-0076	• 1 BR apt. • sm. backyard • $700/mo., 1st/last • pkg. avail. Mrs. Ryder, 689-3645

1. What's the location of the $1,000 apartment? _____

   Who pays utilities? _____

2. Is the "ocean view" apartment large or small? _____

   Where is the parking? _____

3. Which apartment has a backyard? _____

   How much is the deposit? _____

B. Choose <u>one</u> apartment. What questions do you have for the landlord? Write your questions below.

Example: *Is the ocean view apartment furnished?* _____

1. _____

2. _____

3. _____

4. _____

5. _____

6. _____

7. _____

8. _____

UNIT 9 | What's Wrong with the Refrigerator ?

Topic: housing problems

Life Skill/Competency: requests to landlords

Structures: *there is/there are; to be*

Vocabulary   The refrigerator/stove/front burner/oven/heater/electricity/lock on the door isn't working.

The toilet/faucet/pipe/drain pipe/ceiling/gas is leaking.

The kitchen sink/toilet/bathroom sink/bathtub is stopped up.

The window is broken.

There are cockroaches/fleas/mice in my apartment.

There's poison on the table.

The window is cracked.

There's medicine on the table.

There are too many plugs.

There's garbage on the floor.

The electric cord is hanging down.

Teaching Suggestions

Activity 1

Refer to the procedure on page v.

Look at page 52 while presenting page 51. Ask *What's the problem here?* about each numbered item in the pictures, eliciting the statements that appear on page 52. (Students may offer other, equally acceptable descriptions of the problem; these should be encouraged.) Reinforce the target vocabulary by relating it to the students' lives, as in the sample presentation of Picture 1 (The refrigerator isn't working.) below.

> Today we're going to talk about problems we sometimes have in our homes. Let's look at the first picture. A lot of things aren't working in this apartment. What does that mean, "aren't working"?…Yes, it means they're broken. Right; it's the same as "don't work." What isn't working in this picture? [pointing]…The refrigerator isn't working. Who has a refrigerator in their house?…I see everyone does. And where is your refrigerator?…In the kitchen. What's the refrigerator used for?…Yes, keeping food cold. Did you ever have a problem with your refrigerator not working?…You did, Thuy?…You were away on vacation for a month? My goodness! Yes, I can imagine the smell. What did you do about it?…

Activity 2

Refer to the procedure on page vi.

Before students start the pairwork, review household fixtures, appliances, and pests. Have pictures of the various objects and animals on hand. One by one, hold them up for students to identify. (Draw simple sketches on the chalkboard if you don't have such pictures on file.) Then write these words at the top of three columns on the chalkboard: *bathroom, kitchen, any room in the house.* Hold up flashcards (which you have made before class) with the names of the fixtures, appliances, and pests, and have students read the words. Have them say which column each item belongs in and tape it to the chalkboard in the correct column.

Then point to the flashcards one by one and give students verbal cues so they can make sentences. For example:

    T: (pointing to the word *toilet*) Stopped up.

    Ss: The toilet is stopped up.

Activity 3

Prepare students for this activity by asking them what's wrong in each of the pictures before you start the tape.

Activity 4

Refer to the procedure on page ix.

After students listen to the conversations, explain that a tenant is anyone who rents an apartment or a house. Then ask all tenants to raise their hands.

In addition, explain that *What's wrong?* is the same as *What's the problem?* and that *I'll take care of it* means *I'll fix it.* Ask students who takes care of problems in their apartment buildings.

Activity 5

Review the intonation patterns for yes/no and *Wh-* questions and introduce the use of rising intonation for requests. As students are listening to the first conversation on tape, write it on the chalkboard. Model the dialogue line by line and ask students whether your voice goes up or down at the end of each sentence. Mark the intonation of statements and *Wh-* questions with falling arrows and yes/no questions and the request with rising arrows. Model the conversation again and have students repeat line by line. If it's helpful, make rising and falling gestures with your hand. Explain that when we ask for something (i.e.,*Would you please look at it today?*), we're making a request, and that requests—like yes/no questions—have rising intonation. Remind students to use the correct intonation when they practice the dialogue with their partners.

After students have completed the second conversation and practiced it with their partners, have two pairs of students perform it for the class.

For further practice asking for help with apartment problems, refer to Expansion Activity 1.

Activity 6

Look at page 56 while presenting page 55. Ask these two questions about each of the numbered details in the picture.

> What's wrong here? [Elicit the statements that appear on page 56.]
>
> Why is this a problem?

Reinforce the new language by relating it to the students' homes, as in the following sample presentation for item 1 (poison on the table).

> Today we're going to talk about being safe at home. What is "safe"?...Yes, it means you don't hurt yourself. For example, do children play in the street?...No; that's not safe. They can get hurt. Now, let's look at this picture. Where is this?...Yes, it's a kitchen. And what's this on the table? [pointing]...Is it milk or poison?...Yes, it's poison. What is poison?...It makes you sick if you eat it....Maybe you will die. How do you know it's poison?...By the picture [pointing to skull and crossbones]. What's an example of poison?... Well, is gasoline a poison?...Yes. What else?...Yes, bleach is a poison. Now, where is this poison?...It's on the table. Is that safe?...Of course not. It's...yes, it's dangerous. "Dangerous" is the opposite of "safe." Why is this dangerous?...Because a child might drink it. Do you keep poisons on the table of your kitchen, Chun?...Good! I'm glad to hear it!

Activity 8

Refer to the procedure on page ix.

After you practice the conversations with the students, explain that the sentences *That's not safe* and *That's dangerous* mean the same thing. Then contrast the words *safe* and *dangerous*. Write them on the chalkboard and instruct students to listen to what you say and state whether the action is safe or dangerous. Here are some phrases you may use.

Children playing in the street	People driving fast
Children playing in the backyard	People walking on the sidewalk
Children using knives	One person walking alone at night
Children drinking milk	People locking their doors at night
Children drinking medicine without their parents at home	People leaving their doors unlocked

Activity 9

After students have read Ken's note to Mr. White, ask these questions to check their comprehension.

Who's the note to?; What apartment does Ken live in?; What is Ken's phone number?;

What's the problem in his apartment?; What does he want the manager to do?;

Does Ken sign only his first name or his full name?; What's the date?

Activity 10

Prepare students for this activity by asking them questions about problems they have or have had with things at home.

After students have completed the conversation and practiced it with their partners, have several pairs of students perform their dialogues for the class.

Encourage students to refer to Ken's note on page 57 as they write to their managers and landlords. As they write their notes, circulate to make sure their notes are complete.

For more practice talking about problems at home, refer to Expansion Activities 2 and 3.

Expansion Activities

1. Strip Story. Using the dialogue on page 54 of the Student Book as a model, type out a new dialogue and cut it into strips of paper, with one strip per line of text. Put students into pairs and give each pair all of the strips necessary to create the dialogue. (The strips should not be in order.) Ask students to arrange the strips to create a conversation. Then have them practice the conversation aloud.

2. Dictate the following sentences and have students write them on a piece of paper. Say each sentence three times.

There are mice in my apartment.	There's garbage on the floor.
The ceiling is leaking.	The toilet is stopped up.
The window is cracked.	There are too many plugs.
There's poison on the table.	The electric cord is hanging down.
The refrigerator isn't working.	The faucet is leaking.

   After students have finished writing, have volunteers write the sentences on the chalkboard.

3. Put students in groups of four or five, and tell them to close their books. At the top of three columns on the chalkboard, write the following phrases: *problems in the kitchen, problems in the bathroom, problems anywhere in the house.* Have students copy these phrases at the top of a sheet of paper. Then give them ten minutes to work with other members of their group and write down as many problems as they can think of in each of the three columns. Encourage them to include problems that aren't mentioned in their books. After ten minutes, have students read the items from their lists out loud. Make a complete list of problems on the chalkboard.

A. On weekdays, Ivan works at the Ace Bicycle Factory. On Saturdays, he works as a handyman for the Sea View Apartments on Green Street. Read the apartment manager's note to Ivan.

Dear Ivan,   November 27

Here's a list of problems we're having now.

The lady in Apt. 18 smells gas in her kitchen. Can you please take care of this right away? The people in Apt. 3 can't use their toilet. It won't flush. Please take care of this too. In Apt. 7, there's no light. Please check the electricity. The woman in Apt. 2 can't do any cooking. Can you please look at her stove? Water is coming through the ceiling in Apt. 44. Please fix the leak. Apt. 32 is cold. It isn't getting any heat. Please check on this. The people in Apt. 27 are having problems with their bathtub. The water goes down very slowly. Please see what you can do about it. The people in Apt. 15 can't lock their back door. Please fix it. The man in Apt. 20 says he sees cockroaches in the kitchen at night. Please take care of this. Finally, in Apt. 11, the bathroom window is cracked. Can we get some new glass?

I hope you can take care of all these things today. If you need me, I'll be back at 1:00.

Sincerely,
Jeff Banks, Apt. Manager

B. Write sentences about the apartment problems.

1. Apt. 2   **The stove isn't working.** _____

2. Apt. 3 _____

3. Apt. 7 _____

4. Apt. 11 _____

5. Apt. 15 _____

6. Apt. 18 _____

7. Apt. 20 _____

8. Apt. 27 _____

9. Apt. 32 _____

10. Apt. 44 _____

UNIT 10 Do You Ever Use a Credit Card?

Topic: shopping

Life Skill/Competency: inquiring about merchandise

Structure: present tense

Vocabulary

use a credit card	go to garage sales	return clothes
worry about money	shop at department stores	steal things
write checks	borrow money	shop at thrift stores
buy flowers	buy red socks	lose your money
picture ID	driver's license	receipt

Teaching Suggestions
Activity 1

Refer to the procedure on page v.

When you ask about the first picture during the presentation, write *Do you ever...?* on the chalkboard and explain that this means, *Do you sometimes...?* (Then erase the words from the chalkboard.) If necessary, remind students of the two answers to this question: *Yes, I do,* and *No, I don't,* and tell them that we can also answer, *No, never.*

Ask questions like the following to present the pictures.

Do you ever _____?

How often do you _____?

Where/When do you _____?

Why do you _____?

The following is a sample presentation of Picture 1 (use a credit card).

> Now let me ask you: Do you ever use a credit card? Well, first of all, what is a credit card? Who has one? Hold it up...Joaquín has a VISA card. That's a credit card...And Elena has a Mastercard. That's a credit card, too. Now when do you use a credit card?...Yes, when you go shopping. And why do you use a credit card?...Yes, when you don't have money with you...Or you don't want to carry money. So, Elena, where do you use your credit card?...At Macy's, when you buy clothes. And what do you have to show when you use your credit card?...Yes, you show ID...And you sign your name. Joaquín, how often do you use your credit card?...Oh, not very much. You like to pay cash.

Grammar Box (page 61 of Student Book, top)

Refer to the procedure on page viii.

Have students practice yes/no questions and short answers. Supply cues by saying a familiar verb phrase, and then call on two students. Student 1 asks the question and Student 2 replies. For example:

T: Buy tools. Jaime and Xuong.

J: Do you ever buy tools?

X: Yes, I do.

Here are some phrases to use.

buy tools	buy used things	read magazines	take naps
sing	sweep the floor	wash the dishes	iron clothes
fix your car	go to museums	go to the library	call your landlord

Activity 4

Before students practice the conversations, call attention to the *How often?* box. To help students distinguish between these expressions of frequency, make sentences and ask questions about your habits. Have students respond with *a lot, once in a while,* or *not very much.* For example:

I go to the library every day. How often is that?

I go to museums once a month. How often is that?

I go to church twice a year. How often is that?

Grammar Box (page 61 of Student Book, bottom)

Refer to the procedure on page viii.

Give students cues from page 60 and have them make statements about themselves using the expressions of frequency in the grammar box. For example:

T: Return clothes, Lourdes.

L: I don't return clothes very much.

Activity 5

After students finish the writing task, have them share some of their sentences with the class.

Grammar Box (page 62 of Student Book, top)

Refer to the procedure on page viii.

Ask individual students yes/no questions. Have them respond and then ask the same questions of other students. For example:

T: Do you like television, Danielle?

D: Yes, I do. Do you like television, Huyen?

H: No, I don't.

Explain that *Do you like* is followed by the name for a thing and *Do you like to* is followed by an action. Ask students to call out the names for other things and list them on the chalkboard. Then have the class call out some actions and write them in another list on the chalkboard. Point out that the actions must be stated in the simple form (*swim* or *run*) and *not* the *-ing* form. Continue the practice with these new noun and verb phrases.

Activity 6

After you practice the conversations with the students, explain that *Me too* is a rejoinder used when two people are making the same affirmative statement, and that *Me neither* is used when two people are making the same negative statement, that is, they are used when both people have the *same* answer. They cannot be used when people have different answers.

In addition, review intonation patterns and teach the concept of primary stress in sentences. Write all three conversations on the chalkboard. Model them line by line, asking students which word is loudest in each sentence and whether your voice goes up or down at the end. Mark the primary stress with a dot and the intonation with rising and falling arrows.

Do you like to go shopping?
Yes, I do.
Me too.

Do you like American food?
No, I don't.
Me neither.

Do you like to eat at restaurants?
Yes, I do.
I don't.

Explain that in sentences, one word is generally spoken louder than the others, and that it's usually at or near the end of the sentence. Practice the dialogues with the students using the correct stress and intonation. Then erase the chalkboard. Help students use the correct stress and intonation as they do the pairwork.

Grammar Box (page 62 of Student Book, bottom)

Refer to the procedure on page viii.

Give students noun and verb cues and have them make statements about themselves. For example:

    T: Hot dogs, Danai.
    D: I don't like hot dogs.
    T: Rent videos, Thuy.
    Th: I like to rent videos.

For reinforcement of yes/no questions and answers in the present tense, refer to Expansion Activity 1.

Activity 7

After students finish the writing task, have them share some of their sentences with the class.

Activities 8 and 9

Refer to the procedure on page x.

For more practice calling stores, refer to Expansion Activity 2.

Activity 10

When you introduce the first two vocabulary items, ask the students with picture ID's and driver's licenses to hold them up. Ask what the difference is. When you introduce *receipt*, ask students where and when they get receipts.

After students listen to the conversation, explain that *I'd like* is a polite way of saying *I want*.

Give students practice using the words *cash, check*, and *credit card* by asking how they pay for various things such as food, clothing, haircuts, rent, and cars.

Activity 11

After students have written and practiced their conversations, have pairs of students perform their dialogues for the class.

Expansion Activities

1. Review yes/no questions and answers with *Do you ever ... ?* with a mingling activity in which students move around the room asking their classmates questions. Pass out copies of (or have students copy from the chalkboard) the following form.

Find 3 people who go to garage sales.	Find 3 people who use a credit card.
1. _____	1. _____
2. _____	2. _____
3. _____	3. _____
Find 3 people who buy flowers.	Find 3 people who shop at thrift stores.
1. _____	1. _____
2. _____	2. _____
3. _____	3. _____

Before starting the activity, read the instructions with the students and model the task. Circulate and ask several students if they go to garage sales. Write the names of those who answer in the affirmative on your form. Remind students to use correct intonation as they ask and answer questions. Then have all students stand up and begin interviewing their classmates.

2. Write on the chalkboard this list of items that might or might not be found at a department store.

work gloves	coffee pots	pliers	children's slippers
cookbooks	telephones	men's boots	brooms

Have students copy the list. Tell them to look up the telephone number for a local department store and call to find out if the store has the items and, if so, on which floor. Tell them to ask questions using these cues.

Do you sell _____? What floor are they on?

Then have students write eight sentences like these and hand them in as homework.

Men's boots are on the first floor of Nelson's Department Store.

There are no brooms at Nelson's Department Store.

A. **Read Xiaoping's letter to her parents in China. Then write the things she likes about the United States under *Likes* and the things she doesn't like under *Dislikes*.**

Dear Mom and Dad,   December 8

Hello! How are you? I miss you a lot! I'm studying hard, and I'm learning a lot about American culture.

In general, I'm happy with my life here. I like my English teachers, but I don't like the size of my classes. There are forty-five students in each class! The counselors at school are nice and helpful. I like them a lot. There are computers at school too, and I like to work on them. I'm writing this letter on a computer right now! But I don't like the vending machines. Sometimes I put in my money and nothing comes out!

Speaking of food, I like American supermarkets. You can buy everything there. But I don't like American food. There's too much fat in it!

Do I like the city? Well, on my way to school, I walk across Milford Bridge. I don't like the bridge. There's too much traffic on it, and it's very noisy. But my neighborhood is nice. There are lots of flowers and trees. I don't really like my apartment, though. It's too small, and there aren't many windows.

There's one more thing I like about life in the United States. I like to go to garage sales! People put the things they don't want out in their garages. Everything is very cheap!

Love,
Xiaoping

Likes	Dislikes
English teachers	

B. **Complete the questions and write short answers about yourself.**

1. __Do__ __you__ __like__ to eat American food?   _____

2. _____ _____ _____ to shop at supermarkets?   _____

3. Do you like _____ _____ to garage sales?   _____

4. _____ _____ _____ to use vending machines?   _____

 **What Does Ken Do on Weeknights?**

Topic: leisure activities

Life Skill/Competency: telephone messages

Structure: present tense

Vocabulary

read books	go to church	run in the park	watch TV
play cards	relax	not do anything	play with (their) friends
play soccer	go dancing	do homework	not do anything

Teaching Suggestions

Activity 1

Refer to the procedure on page v.

Before beginning the presentation, remind students that we use *does* and *do* to ask about things that people *usually* or *sometimes* (i.e., habitually) do.

Ask questions like the following to present the pictures.

What does (Ken) usually do on weeknights?

Do you ever _____?

Do you enjoy _____ing?

How often do you _____?

Where do you _____?

Who do you _____ with?

The following is a sample presentation of Picture 1 (read books).

> Today we're going to talk about what people do in their leisure time. What is "leisure time"?...Yes, it's our free time. When do we have leisure time?...On Sunday...After work...During vacation. Now, look at these letters [pointing to MTWTh]. What are they?...Yes, Monday, Tuesday, Wednesday, Thursday. Daytime or nighttime [pointing to the moon]?...Nighttime. These are what we call "weeknights." What are weeknights, then?...Right. Now, let's talk about Ken. What does he do on weeknights?...He reads books. Any idea what kind of books he reads?...Maybe adventure stories...Maybe love stories. Do any of you read books on weeknights?...

Grammar Box (page 66 of Student Book)

Refer to the procedure on page viii.

Give students practice adding the third-person *-s*. Ask individuals questions and have the class report what they say. For example:

    T: Do you like to shop at department stores, Milagros?

    M: Yes, I do.

    T: What do you buy there?

    M: Blue jeans.

    T: What does Milagros do at department stores, class?

    Ss: She buys blue jeans.

You may ask about shopping at various other types of stores—thrift shops, hardware stores, supermarkets, candy shops—and about what students read at libraries, what they do at museums, and what they do at the park.

Activity 4

If students need additional practice writing the third-person singular form of verbs, put the following verbs on the chalkboard and have them add -s or -es.

weigh	measure	do	copy	type
say	brush	ask	kiss	use
cry	like	touch	sing	leave

In addition, teach students that the long and short endings on third-person singular verbs are governed by the same rules as the endings on plural nouns. Help students recall the rules. First, say these pairs of verbs aloud, clapping out the syllables: *read/reads, play/plays, like/likes, fix/fixes, miss/misses, wash/washes.* Go through the pairs of verbs again, having students clap and repeat after you. Then write *long sound* and *short sound* at the top of two columns on one side of the chalkboard and the following list of verbs on the other side of the chalkboard.

sweep	teach	cut	dry	park
wash	play	press	weigh	throw
study	watch	buy	kiss	leave
wait	fix	work	touch	live

Point to the verbs one by one and say both the simple and the third-person singular forms. Have students tell you whether both forms of the verb have the same number of syllables or whether the third-person singular form has an extra syllable. Write each verb in the appropriate column. After all of the verbs have been written in the correct column, circle the verb endings that require an additional syllable—*ch, x, sh,* and *s.* Explain that like nouns, verbs ending with the sounds /ch/, /j,/ /s/, /sh/, /x/, and /z/ will have an additional syllable in the third-person singular form. Point to the verbs again and have students pronounce the third-person singular forms.

Grammar Box (page 67 of Student Book, middle)

Refer to the procedure on page viii.

Divide the class in half and tell half of the students they'll be asking a question and the other half they'll be making an answer. Then ask individual students what they usually do at various times during the week. Have the class repeat this question and answer in the third person. For example:

> T: What do you usually do on Monday mornings, Muu?
>
> M: I work.
>
> Ss1: What does he usually do on Monday mornings?
>
> Ss2: He works.

Grammar Box (page 68 of Student Book, top)

Refer to the procedure on page viii.

Draw the following chart on the chalkboard. Have students copy the chart, writing the names for family members and friends down the left side and copying the actions across the top.

family members/ friends	drive a car	clean the house	read magazines	take naps
(mother)				
(son)				

Have students fill in the chart with *yes* and *no*. Then have them make statements about members of their family, such as *My husband takes a nap in the afternoon.*

Activity 6

After students finish the writing task, have a few students share a sentence with the class before all students close their books and begin talking with their partners.

Grammar Box (page 68 of Student Book, middle)

Refer to the procedure on page viii.

Tell students to refer to the charts they made for the activity above. Have them make sentences using *likes to* and *doesn't like to* about family members and friends.

Activity 7

After students finish the writing task, have a few students share a sentence with the class before all students close their books and begin talking with their partners.

For reinforcement of leisure activities, refer to Expansion Activity 1. For reinforcement of the third-person singular *-s*, refer to Expansion Activity 2.

Activities 8 and 9

Refer to the procedure on page x.

After students listen to the conversation, explain that *Would you like...?* is a polite way of asking *Do you want...?*

Activity 11

After students have completed the conversation and improvised some new conversations, have pairs of students perform their dialogues for the class.

Expansion Activities

1. To review and expand on leisure activities, have the class play "Leisure Time Bingo." (The only thing you'll need to prepare is lots of counters, coins, or little paper squares that students can use to cover up the squares on their bingo cards, which they will make in class.)

   First, have the class brainstorm for as many leisure activities as they can think of. Write all of these activities on the chalkboard. Then have each student take out a piece of paper and draw a grid five squares across and five squares down. Tell students to copy a leisure activity from the chalkboard in each square. It's important for students to understand that they are not to write the activities in any particular order, since no two bingo cards should look the same. You may need to demonstrate how to do this by drawing two example bingo cards on the chalkboard. When the bingo cards are finished, begin the game. Call out sentences containing the various leisure activities, as follows.

   I *visit friends* on the weekend.   I often *go dancing* at Club 39.

   Write down the leisure activities as you call them out. The first student to get five leisure activities in a row or on the diagonal wins the game. Prizes may be awarded, but you may want to check for accuracy by comparing students' bingo cards with your notes before giving out the prizes. The game may be played several times.

2. To review the use of the third person *-s*, dictate the following paragraph and have students write it down sentence by sentence.

   Linda and Paul do a lot of things during the week. They go to school from 8:30 A.M. to 3:00 P.M. On Monday and Wednesday afternoons, they play with their friends. They have a lot of fun. On Tuesday and Thursday afternoons, they swim at a pool near the house. Most nights, they wash the dishes with their father. They do their homework too. But on Friday nights, they watch TV.

   To check for accuracy, have volunteers write the paragraph on the chalkboard. Then have students rewrite the paragraph in the third-person singular, beginning with either *Linda* or *Paul*. When students finish writing, collect their papers.

Read about Mr. Sato's weekly activities. Then write answers to the questions below. Write complete sentences.

Mr. Sato is a busy man. He's the owner of the Ace Bicycle Factory, and he works very hard. He's at the factory from 8:00 A.M. to 6:00 P.M. Monday to Saturday.

In the evenings, he does different things. On Monday and Thursday, he runs in the park with his neighbor, Mr. Jones. On Tuesday and Friday, he visits his mother. On Wednesday, he stays home and reads magazines. On Saturday, he and his wife play cards with Mr. and Mrs. Jones.

On Sundays, Mr. Sato relaxes. In the morning, his wife goes to church, but he doesn't do anything. When Mrs. Sato comes home, the two of them work in the garden. Later in the afternoon, Mr. Sato sometimes goes to museums and looks at pictures. At night, he and his wife watch TV.

Mrs. Sato worries about her husband. She thinks he does too many things. But Mr. Sato is only happy when he's busy. So he goes to bed early, eats good food, and takes a lot of vitamins so his wife will be happy too.

1. What does Mr. Sato do on weekdays?

    _____

2. What does he do on Wednesday evenings?

    _____

3. How often does he visit his mother?

    _____

4. What nights does Mr. Sato come home very tired?

    _____

5. What does he do on Sunday mornings?

    _____

6. Why does Mrs. Sato worry about her husband?

    _____

 **UNIT 12** # What Does Judy Do?

Topic: occupations

Life Skill/Competency: finding out about jobs

Structure: present tense

Vocabulary
secretary/receptionist—type letters and answer phones
construction worker—build houses and buildings
stock clerk—put things on shelves
seamstress—sew clothes
factory worker—work in a factory
mail carrier—deliver mail
fire fighter—put out fires
police officer—protect citizens
plumber—fix pipes
mechanic—repair cars and machines
janitor—clean offices and buildings
electrician—work with electricity
cashier—take money and give change
waitress/waiter—serve food
security guard—guard stores and banks
dentist—take care of our teeth

Teaching Suggestions
Activity 1

Refer to the procedure on page v.

When you ask what the various people do in their jobs, students' responses needn't be restricted to those listed on page 72. The captions on page 72 are for students' reference, but appropriate variations or expansions are to be encouraged.

Ask questions like the following to present the pictures.

What is this person's job?

Where does a _____ work?

What does a _____ do?

Do you know a _____?

Is any of you a _____?

What does a _____ wear?

The following is a sample presentation of Picture 1 (secretary/receptionist).

> Today we're going to talk about people's jobs. Look at Judy. What does she do?...She's a secretary. Also, she helps people who visit the office. Do you know what we call that person?...Well, is she a teacher or a receptionist?...She's a receptionist. Can you say that?...Now, where does a secretary or receptionist work?...In an office. And what does a secretary or receptionist do?...Yes, a secretary types letters. What else?...Yes, a receptionist answers the telephone. What else?...Yes, a receptionist answers your questions when you go to the office. Now, is any of you a secretary or receptionist, or were you in your country?...You were, Olga? What did you do as a receptionist?...

Activity 2

Refer to the procedure on page vi.

Write all of the occupations on the chalkboard. As you model the pronunciation of each, ask which word/syllable is the loudest. Mark the loudest syllable with a dot.

sécretary   constrúction worker   stóck clerk   séamstress

(Many of these occupations are compound nouns; the stressed syllable occurs in the first noun.) As students repeat after you, help them stress the noun phrases correctly.

Give students more practice with the vocabulary before they do the pairwork. Mime the tasks performed by people in the various occupations and engage students in dialogues like the following.

> T: (miming sewing a piece of clothing)
>
>   What am I?
>
> Ss: A seamstress.
>
> T: What am I doing?
>
> Ss: Sewing clothes.

Activity 6

Prepare students for the writing task by asking them about their jobs and duties and the jobs of family members and friends. For example:

> T: What do you do, Joaquín?
>
> J: I'm a construction worker. I build houses.
>
> T: And do you have a brother?
>
> J: Yes, I do.
>
> T: What does he do?
>
> J: He's a mechanic. He fixes cars.

Help students identify occupations they or their family members may have that are not presented in this unit. Write these occupations on the chalkboard.

After students finish writing, have them share some of their sentences with the class.

For reinforcement of jobs and duties, refer to Expansion Activities 1 and 2.

Activity 7

Circulate as students work through this activity, urging them to skip items they don't know. After they've written out as many of the abbreviations as they can with their partners, have volunteers write them on the chalkboard. Spell out the words for any abbreviations students are unfamiliar with, and then go through and clarify the meanings of all the abbreviations.

Activity 8

After students have finished writing answers to the questions, check their work by having volunteers write the answers on the chalkboard.

Activity 10

After students share their qualifications with their partners, have some students share their qualifications with the class.

For more practice with Help Wanted ads, refer to Expansion Activity 3.

Expansion Activities

1. To review the different occupations, read each of the short conversations (on the next page) aloud and have students guess the occupation of the significant speaker. To indicate when the speaker changes, use dolls or puppets, or draw two stick figures on the chalkboard and point to them as you speak.

A: Is there any mail for me today?

B: Yes, sir. There are two letters and a magazine.

A: Where should I put this box?

B: Put it on the top shelf, next to the water heater.

A: What's wrong, ma'am?

B: The lights are out in the kitchen and the bedroom.

A: How can I get inside the shopping center?

B: I'm sorry, sir, but the shopping center is closed now. Come back tomorrow morning at 10:00.

A: There's water all over the bathroom floor!

B: Hmm. It looks like your toilet is leaking.

A: I'm sorry, sir, but your car isn't finished yet.

B: What?

A: We still have to repair the front seat.

A: You're working on an office building now, right?

B: Yes. It's a building with 36 floors.

A: Where's the fire, ma'am?

B: It's upstairs in the bedroom.

A: OK. Get everyone out of the house. We're coming in right now.

A: Are the new dresses ready yet?

B: No, they aren't. I'm sewing a pair of pants now.

A: Evans Law Offices. May I help you?

B: May I please speak to Mr. Evans?

A: Just a minute, please.

2. Bring in a set of notecards (which you have made before class) with the names of the occupations. Hand students one card apiece and have them take turns going to the front of the classroom and miming their occupations. Have the rest of the class guess the occupations and practice talking about job duties by asking yes/no questions. For example:

Ss: Are you a stock clerk?

S: No, I'm not.

Ss: Are you a plumber?

S: Yes, I am.

Ss: Do you fix pipes?

S: Yes, I do.

3. Photocopy some Help Wanted ads from your local newspaper. Pass these out to the students and have them rewrite the ads with their partners, spelling out the abbreviated words. Then ask them questions about the jobs. For example:

Is the cashier job full time or part time?; What's the salary?; What do you do if you want the receptionist job?; How much experience is required?

A. **Read the two stories. Then rewrite them using *he, she, his*, and *her*.**

1. My name is Tran Ng. I'm a cashier at Dan's Supermarket. I stand at the counter and weigh the fruit and vegetables. Then I take people's money and give them change. I'm moving next month, and I want a new job. I have two years' experience. I speak English, Vietnamese, and Chinese.

<u>Her name is Tran Ng. She's</u> _____

_____

_____

_____

_____

2. My name is Joe Anderson. I'm a mechanic, and I want a full-time job. Right now, I have a part-time job at A-1 Auto Works. I fix American cars there. But I can repair foreign cars too. I have my own tools, and I have six years' experience. I can start work anytime.

_____

_____

_____

_____

_____

B. **Read these Help Wanted ads. Would Tran and Joe want any of these jobs and have the right qualifications for them? Write their names below the jobs they can do and might want.**

CASHIER for Alba's Grocery, 202 Pike. No exp. nec. Must speak Spanish.	**CASHIER** for Bob's Market, 1 yr. exp. req. Call Bob at 527-8975.	**MECHANIC**. Mr. Fix-It. Exp. req. Foreign & American cars. 622-8564.	**MECHANIC**. Temp P/T work, Mo's Car Repair. Must have tools. 829-7562.
_____	_____	_____	_____

UNIT 13 Can You Drive a Truck?

Topic: work skills

Life Skill/Competency: calling for a job interview

Structure: modal *can*

Vocabulary

drive a truck	use a computer	alter clothes
use a calculator	repair machines	use a cash register
type	use hand tools	change a tire
read maps	use electric tools	fool your boss

Teaching Suggestions

Activity 1

Refer to the procedure on page v.

If necessary during the presentation, help students with the answers, *Yes, I can* and *No, I can't.*

Ask questions like the following to present the pictures.

Can you _____?

Can anyone in your family _____?

Do you ever _____ at work?

How often do you _____?

Where/When did you learn to _____?

Do you enjoy _____ing?

The following is a sample presentation of Picture 1 (drive a truck).

> Today we're going to talk about things we can or can't do. Sergio, can you drive a truck?...No, you can't. What about you, Jaime?...You can? Do you drive a truck at work?...You do. A big one or a small one?...A big truck. Where did you learn to drive a truck?...Your father taught you. And you, Xiao Lin, can you drive a truck?...You can. Do you drive a truck at work?...You did back in China. Did you enjoy it?...Not very much, huh? Yes, driving a truck is hard work.

Activity 2

Refer to the procedure on page vi.

After students do the pairwork, give them additional practice with the new vocabulary while reviewing and expanding upon the occupations in Unit 12. Ask students to name the occupations of people who can do each task on this page. Supply the names of occupations that students don't know. For example:

T: Who can type?

Ss: A secretary.

T: Who can repair office machines?

Ss: (no answer)

T: A repair person.

Grammar Box (page 79 of Student Book)

Refer to the procedure on page viii.

Supply cues and have one student ask a question and another student respond. For example:

T: Sing, Greta and Suhua.

G: Can you sing?

S: Yes, I can.

Use these cues: *sing, dance, play soccer, sew, fix pipes, cook, speak French, play cards.*

Activity 5

Prepare students for the writing task by inquiring about their skills and helping them make statements with *can*. For example:

T: Can you cook, Van Thu?

V: Yes, I can.

T: What kind of food?

V: I can cook Vietnamese food.

After students finish the writing task, have two students share an affirmative and a negative sentence with the class. Write these statements on the chalkboard and teach the difference between the pronunciation of *can* and *can't* in statements. In each affirmative statement, cross out the word *can* and above it write *kn*, and put a dot above the main verb and other stressed syllables. In each negative statement, put a dot above *can't* and other stressed syllables, as follows.

I ~~can~~ cook Vietnamese food.   I can't fix cars.

I ~~can~~ speak three languages.   I can't use a computer.

Explain that the difference in the pronunciation of *can* and *can't* in statements isn't the final *t* in *can't*, which is often dropped. What distinguishes the two is the fact that the word *can't* receives stress and the vowel is pronounced fully, while the word *can* is unstressed and in it the vowel is reduced. Have students repeat these sentences with the correct stress and vowel sounds. Then ask students to continue making statements about themselves, and have the class repeat each sentence to practice the pronunciation of *can* and *can't*.

Grammar Box (page 80 of Student Book)

Refer to the procedure on page viii.

Explain that *know how to* has the same meaning as *can*. Practice the new structure by supplying cues and having one student ask a question and another student respond. For example:

T: Speak Spanish. Lan and Manuel.

L: Do you know how to speak Spanish?

M: Yes, I do.

Use these cues: *sing, dance, play soccer, sew, fix pipes, cook, speak French, play cards.*

Activity 7

Prepare students for the writing task by inquiring about their skills and helping them make statements with *know how to*. For example:

T: Do you know how to fix cars, Luong?

L: Yes, I do.

T: What kind of cars?

L: I know how to fix VW's.

T: How many years' experience do you have?

L: I have nine years' experience.

After students finish writing, have them share some of their sentences, both affirmative and negative, with the class.

For more practice stating job skills, refer to Expansion Activity 1.

Activities 8 and 9

Refer to the procedure on page x.

Prepare students for the activities on pages 81 and 82 by asking these questions.

If you see a Help Wanted ad and you want the job, what do you do?;

When you call, what do they usually ask you to do next?

Activity 10

After students have written their conversations and practiced them with their partners, have several pairs of students perform their dialogues for the class.

For more practice calling about jobs, refer to Expansion Activity 2.

Expansion Activities

1. To review the vocabulary for talking about skills, mime the different actions and have students guess what you're doing. Then hold up flashcards (which you have made before class) with verb phrases such as *alter clothes* and *use hand tools*, and have students read the phrases aloud. After the class reads the phrase, ask two or three students if they have that skill. Use *can* or *know how to* in your questions.

   Then draw a chart on the chalkboard with four columns and nine rows, and have students copy the chart. Tell students to leave the first row empty. Then dictate eight skills for the students to write in the left column in rows 2 through 9. Tell them they will interview three classmates about these skills. Then model the task. Write the name of one student at the top of the second column and ask him or her about two or three of the skills. (Use *Can you...* or *Do you know how to...* in your questions.) Write *yes* or *no* in the corresponding boxes. Tell students to choose a partner and ask him or her about all eight of the skills, and then go on to two other classmates, writing their names at the top of columns 3 and 4 and their answers below. Then have students begin interviewing each other.

   When students have filled in their charts, have them write two or three sentences about each classmate and hand them in as homework. For example:

   Juan can drive a truck, but he can't use a computer.

   Ali knows how to repair machines, but he doesn't know how to type.

2. Strip Story. Using the dialogue on page 81 as a model, type out a new dialogue and cut it into strips of paper, with one strip per line of text. Put students into groups of three and give each group all of the strips necessary to create the dialogue. (The strips should not be in order.) Ask students to arrange the strips to create a conversation. Then have them practice the conversation aloud.

A. Sally is looking for a new job. Read her letter to Perry's Imports.

Dear Mr. Perry,   February 12
     I'm writing about the secretarial job advertised in the newspaper yesterday. I'd like to tell you about my work experience and skills.
     I have three years' experience as a secretary. Right now, I'm working as a secretary/receptionist for the Bidwell Company. It's a part-time job. Now I want a full-time job.
     I have many secretarial skills. I can type 60 words a minute. I know how to use a calculator, and I'm fast with the adding machine. I know how to speak English and Spanish, and I can write in those languages too. I don't know how to use a computer, but I learn quickly.
     Right now, I'm taking business classes at Glade Community College. My classes are at night, so I can work in the mornings and in the afternoons. I'd like to meet you and talk about the job. I can come for an interview any afternoon. My phone number is 764-3295. I hope to hear from you.
                                   Sincerely,
                                   Sally Jones

B. Now write answers to the questions. Use the answers in the box.

Yes, she can.   No, she can't.   Yes, she does.   No, she doesn't.

1. Does Sally have experience as a secretary? **Yes, she does.** _____

2. Does she have a job now? _____

3. Does she want a part-time job? _____

4. Can she type? _____

5. Does she know how to use a computer? _____

6. Does she know how to use a calculator? _____

7. Can she speak Japanese? _____

8. Can she write in English and Spanish? _____

9. Can she work at night? _____

10. Can she come for an interview in the afternoon? _____

UNIT 14   Where Does Carlos Work?

Topic: habitual activities

Life Skill/Competency: job interviews

Structure: modal *have to*

Vocabulary

Where does he work?

How does he get to work?

What time does he get to work?

How many days does he work?

How many hours does he work?

How often does he get paid?

What day does he get paid?

What does he do after work?

Who does he relax with?

When does he go shopping?

Where does he go shopping?

What kind of things does he read?

How much time does he read every day?/
How long does he read every day?

How often does he go to the movies?

What kind of movies does he see?

Teaching Suggestions
Activity 1

Refer to the procedure on page v.

Look at page 84 while presenting page 83, asking the questions that appear beside each picture. Ask each question about Carlos first, and then ask the same question of your students. The words and phrases that appear with the pictures are Carlos's answers to the questions, but they also serve as cues for the questions. During the presentation, and again before beginning the pairwork in Activity 3, have volunteers model the questions as the students look at the pictures.

The following is a sample presentation of Picture 1 (Where does Carlos work?).

> Today we're going to talk about what Carlos does at work and in his free time. First, where does he work? [pointing to the answer]...He works at Talbot Construction. What about you, Chau? Where do you work?...At Safeway. And you, Zhen? Where do you work?...At the Comfort Inn. Now, can you make the question? "Where...?" That's right, Van. Anyone else want to make the question?....Good, Maria. Now, can you ask about Carlos? "Where...?" Right. Where does he work?...

After you make the initial presentation of vocabulary with the pictures, ask students to recall all the *Wh-* words they're familiar with, and list these on the chalkboard. Then have students turn to page 84 and proceed with Activity 2.

Activity 4

Before students start the writing task, ask three or four students about their partners' habits at work and during their free time, and have them make sentences aloud.

After students have finished writing, have them share some of their sentences with the class.

For reinforcement of question formation, refer to the Expansion Activity.

Activity 5

Prepare students for the reading task by familiarizing them with some of the new vocabulary before they start to read. List the following items on the chalkboard: *have to, in person, appointment, fill out, application form, employer.* Point to these expressions one by one as you ask students the questions on the next page.

If you want to come to school here, what do you have to *do?; Do you* have to *enroll in a class?; How do you enroll?; Can you enroll on the telephone, or do you* have to *come to school in person?; Can you enroll anytime, or do you have to make an appointment to see a counselor?; What do you* have to fill out, *a registration form or an* application form*?; When do you* have to fill out *an application form?; Do you* have to *ask your* employer *about coming to school here?*

After students have written answers to the questions in their books, check their comprehension by having volunteers write the answers on the chalkboard.

Activity 6

Have students close their books. Then ask a few individuals questions like these to help students get started on the speaking task.

What do you have to do if you want a job in El Salvador, María?; And what do you have to do next?; What do you have to do after that?; Is there anything else you have to do?

Activity 7

Ask a student to read the example of what children have to and don't have to do. Then ask students to state one thing adults have to do and one thing they don't have to do, and write these on the chalkboard. Then put students in groups of four and have them list as many activities as they can. After they finish, ask them to share their activities aloud; write the activities on the board in four columns, one column apiece for what children and adults have to and don't have to do. Continue until students have shared all of the activities on their lists.

Before students start the writing task, have several of them respond to these questions.

What do you have to do at work?; Do you have to wear nice clothes at work?; What do you have to do for your family?; Do you have to earn all of the money for your family?; What do you have to do on Sundays?; Do you have to work on Sundays?

When students have finished writing, ask one student to share an affirmative and a negative sentence he or she wrote. Put these on the chalkboard, and teach the pronunciation of *have to* in informal speech. Cross out the words *have to* and above them write *hafta.* Explain that this is often the pronunciation of *have to* in spoken English. Have students repeat the two sentences until they are pronouncing the auxiliary correctly. Then say these verb phrases one by one—*work, clean the house, wash the dishes, sweep the floor, fix the car, type a letter, do my homework*—and call on students to make sentences like these.

I *hafta* work.

I don't *hafta* clean the house.

Ask other students to share their sentences with the class, and help them with their pronunciation of *hafta.*

Activity 10

After students read the Help Wanted ad, ask these questions.

What kind of job is it?; Is it full time or part time?; How old does the person have to be?;

What else does the person have to do?; What kind of store is it?; What's the address?

Activity 11

To prepare students for the writing task, tell them that you are looking for another teaching job. Have students pretend to be the directors of a school and ask you some interview questions aloud. Respond appropriately.

Activity 12

Before students fill out the form, read through it with them, encouraging them to ask questions about words or expressions they don't understand.

Expansion Activity

For a challenging review of question formation, make an overhead transparency of the following chart and have the students play *Jeopardy*. In addition to this transparency, you'll need 30 counters or squares of paper to cover the answers.

	SHOPPING	WORK	HOUSING	COMMUNITY RESOURCES	LEISURE ACTIVITIES
25 POINTS	It's down the hall to the left.	It's on the top shelf next to the sponges.	No, it isn't. It's unfurnished.	They're at the day-care center.	On the weekends, I go dancing.
50 POINTS	Because she needs some new clothes.	I'm a mail carrier.	It's $800 a month.	It opens at 10:00 A.M.	I go to the movies every Saturday night.
75 POINTS	Yes, we do. They're on the third floor.	'No, it isn't. It's part time.	There are 2 bedrooms.	I was at the hospital visiting a friend.	I play cards with my parents.
100 POINTS	No. I never steal things.	I have five years' experience.	The landlord pays the utilities.	Because he's looking for work.	I read love stories.
150 POINTS	I'm paying for this with cash.	No, I can't, but I learn quickly.	The drain pipe is leaking.	Yes. The number is 967-3231.	He plays from 1:00 to 4:00.
200 POINTS	No, we don't. We take cash or checks.	She works six days a week.	Sure. I can stop by at 5:00.	Yes, there is. It's on the corner of First and Main.	No, she doesn't. She likes to shop downtown.

To play the game, put the transparency on the overhead projector and cover all the answers with markers before turning on the projector. (If you don't have an overhead projector, the same chart can be drawn on the chalkboard and each question covered with a piece of paper.)

1. Divide the class into two or more teams and number the members of each team.

2. A member of one team chooses a topic and the number of points. (The more difficult questions are awarded a greater number of points.)

3. He or she must ask a question that corresponds to the answer for the topic and number of points chosen. If the answer contains the pronoun *he, she, it,* or *they,* the question should be formulated using an appropriate noun. For example, an appropriate question for *He leaves for work at 7:00 A.M.* might be *When does Ken leave for work?*

4. If a student asks an appropriate question, his or her team will be awarded the number of points to the left of the question. If a student asks a question that is not appropriate, a member of another team gets a chance to ask a question.

5. Keep score on the chalkboard.

6. When all of the answers have elicited appropriate questions, the game ends. The team with the most points wins.

A. **Read about what happens at the Gomez house on weekdays.**

At the Gomez house, the day starts at 6:30 in the morning. Carlos and Susan are the first ones up. Susan fixes breakfast. Carlos makes sandwiches for everyone's lunch, and he packs them in four paper bags. Then Linda and Paul get up so the whole family can eat breakfast together. They usually have cereal and toast, but once in a while they have eggs. Then they get dressed. Susan dresses in nice clothes, and Carlos wears workmen's clothes.

Then everybody starts to leave the house. Susan goes first, at 7:40. She takes the car. After Susan leaves, Linda feeds the parrot, and Paul feeds the cat. The cat eats quickly and goes outside to play. The kids leave the house with their father at 8:00. They walk five blocks to school. Then Carlos says good-bye and catches the bus.

The parrot is home alone for most of the day. Once in a while he feels happy and dances in his cage. Most of the time the parrot feels lonely. Then he talks to himself. Sometimes he talks so loud he scares the mail carrier! But he's never lonely in the evening. By 5:30, Carlos, Susan, and the kids are home, and the house is busy again.

B. **Read the answers and write the questions.**

1. What time do Susan and Carlos get up?   At 6:30.

2. _____   Four sandwiches.

3. _____   Cereal and toast.

4. _____   Once in a while.

5. _____   Work clothes.

6. _____   At 7:40.

7. _____   By car.

8. _____   He plays outside.

9. _____   At 8:00.

10. _____   With their father.

11. _____   Most of the time.

12. _____   Nine and a half hours.

 **What's the Matter with Susan?**

Topic: health problems

Life Skill/Competency: giving advice

Structure: present tense

Vocabulary

She has a cold.	He has diarrhea.
He has a cough.	She has a rash.
He has a sore throat./His throat hurts.	He has a toothache./His tooth hurts.
She has the flu/a fever and chills.	She has cramps.
He has an earache./His ear hurts.	She feels dizzy.
She feels sick to her stomach.	He feels run-down.

measles	cavity	shot	pill/tablet	teaspoon
chicken pox	infection	thermometer	capsule	tablespoon

Teaching Suggestions
Activity 1

Refer to the procedure on page v.

You will ask students a question during the presentation that is not answered in the book: *Why does this person have this problem?* Students are to speculate freely.

Ask questions like the following to present the pictures.

What's the problem with this person?

How do you know he/she has a _____?

Why does he/she have a _____? (free speculation)

Do you ever get a _____?

Why/When do you have a _____?

What do you do when you have a _____?

The following is a sample presentation of Picture 1 (She has a cold.).

> Take a look at these people. How do they look to you?...Yes, they're sick. Today we're going to talk about health problems. What's "health"?...Yes, it's our bodies, if we feel sick or healthy. Let's look at Susan. What's the matter with her?...She has a cold. How do you know Susan has a cold?...She's lying in bed...She looks miserable. And why do you think she got this cold? Any ideas?...Yes, maybe she went out without a coat...Or maybe she went out in the rain. Could be. Do you ever get a cold or the flu?...You do, Elena? What do you do when you get a cold?...You rest in bed. What do other people do when they get a cold?...You drink tea?...You have chicken soup?...

Activity 2

Refer to the procedure on page vi.

After students finish the pairwork, give them more practice with the vocabulary. Say a series of sentences, such as *You have an earache* and *Your tooth hurts*, and have students mime the ailments at their seats. Then mime the ailments yourself and have students say what's wrong. Have them use both forms—*You have a/an* _____ and *Your* _____ *hurts*—to describe the health problems pictured in Items 3, 5, and 9. In addition, have students repeat the names of the childhood diseases after you, and explain that both are rashes most children come down with once in their lives.

Activity 4

Refer to the procedure on page ix.

Before practicing the conversations with the students, explain that *since* must be followed by an expression that refers to some time in the past, and put the following examples on the chalkboard.

Since	yesterday
	last weekend
	Monday
	the day before yesterday
	last night

Encourage students to use different past time expressions as they do the pairwork.

Activity 5

Before students do the writing task, involve them in a class discussion in which you ask several students what they do to alleviate each of the illnesses presented in the unit. To teach vocabulary that may come up, have some or all of the following over-the-counter medications on hand: aspirin and other pain relievers, antacids, diarrhea medicines, cough drops, throat lozenges, cortizone ointment or cream, and vitamins. If and when you introduce these medications, ask several students if they use them and what other similar medications they know of. Pass them around the classroom so students have a chance to touch and smell them.

As students write their sentences, circulate and help them with any unfamiliar vocabulary or expressions they may want to use. After students finish writing, have them share some of their sentences with the class.

Activity 6

Refer to the procedure on page ix.

Help students with primary stress and intonation as you practice the conversations. Write the first dialogue on the chalkboard and model it line by line. Have students listen for which word is loudest in each sentence and whether your voice goes up or down at the end. Mark the primary stress with a dot and the intonation with a falling arrow.

I'm not feeling well.

What's the matter?

I have a toothache.

Why don't you see a dentist?

That's a good idea.

I hope you feel better soon.

Help students recall that in English, one word in the sentence is usually spoken louder than the others, and this word is generally at or near the end of the sentence. Also, point out that suggestions such as *Why don't you...?*, like statements and *Wh-* questions, generally have falling intonation. Practice both dialogues with the students using the correct stress and intonation. Then erase the chalkboard. Remind students to use the correct stress and intonation as they do the pairwork.

Activities 7 and 8

Refer to the procedure on page x.

As you present the words *cavity* and *infection*, ask several students if they've had these medical problems and, if so, how they have been taken care of. When you introduce the word *shot*, ask students if they've had shots and why they've had them. When you introduce *thermometer*, ask students if they have thermometers at home and if they use them in their countries. Explain that the "normal" temperature for human beings is about 98.6° Fahrenheit. Any temperature above this will be called "high."

For more practice talking about health problems and medicine, refer to Expansion Activity 1.

Activity 10

After students have written and practiced their conversations and had time to improvise conversations about other health problems, have several pairs of students share their dialogues with the class.

Activities 11 and 12

Information Gap. Refer to the procedure on page xi.

After teaching the vocabulary items, read the labels below with the students. Explain that *dosage* means how much medicine you should take.

After students finish the Information Gap task, ask the A's for information about the labels on the top and the B's for information about the labels on the bottom, and write it on the chalkboard.

For more practice reading medicine labels, refer to Expansion Activity 2.

Expansion Activities

1. To review health problems and common remedies, bring in notecards (which you have made before class) with the names of the illnesses and pass one out to each student in the class. (Two or more students may be given cards with the same illness, depending on the size of the class.) Have students mime their problems in front of the class. The class will say what's wrong and individual students offer medical advice. For example:

    T: What's the matter with Bao Chu?

    Ss: He has a headache.

    T: What can he do about it, Pedro?

    P: Take some aspirin!

2. Type out information from the labels of four over-the-counter medications in your medicine cabinet. Under each "label," write the following phrases and questions.

    Name of medication: _____

    What is it for? _____

    How much is in the bottle? _____

    Dosage for children: _____

    Dosage for adults: _____

    Put students in pairs. Give a copy of the handout to each pair of students. Have students work with their partners to read the labels and fill in the blanks with the missing information. When they've finished the task, have them write the information on the chalkboard.

A. **Read Judy's letter to her friend Debbie. Then look at the pictures of the health problems and write the names of the people below.**

Dear Debbie,   January 23

    Things aren't going very well at the bicycle factory today. It's 10:00 on Thursday morning, and I'm the only one here at work.

    Ken is down with diarrhea. He's taking diarrhea medicine, but still he has to run to the bathroom every few minutes. Isn't that terrible? Ivan's out with the flu. His temperature is 103 degrees! He has a doctor's appointment this afternoon. I hope the doctor gives him some medicine. Ruth is home in bed now. She has cramps. She's taking aspirin every four hours and drinking tea. Poor Ruth. Susan isn't sick, but her daughter, Linda, has the measles! So Susan's at home taking care of Linda. Then Lisa's sick too. She's out with an earache. Maybe she has an infection. Mr. Sato isn't sick, but his wife has a toothache. He thinks she has a cavity, so he's taking her to the dentist today.

    Oh, no! All of a sudden I feel sick to my stomach. Am I feeling bad because I'm writing about these problems, or am I getting sick too? Oh, dear! I hope not!

Love,
Judy

    _____ **Ken**

    _____

B. **Write the health problems people have.**

1. <u>Ken has diarrhea.</u>   4. _____

2. _____   5. _____

3. _____   6. _____

Is Carlos Going to Go to Work on Thursday?

Topic: health problems

Life Skill/Competency: calling in sick

Structure: future *going to*

Vocabulary
check into the hospital	go skiing	eat ice cream
have an operation	feel bad	drink soda
go to work	have a tooth pulled	eat a hamburger
call in sick	stay home	have a stomachache

Teaching Suggestions
Activity 1

Refer to the procedure on page v.

For each of the four story lines on page 99, ask: 1) *what* is going to happen next Tuesday and Wednesday, and 2) *if* the depicted action is going to happen on Thursday. (This will be a matter of speculation.) Use the expression *going to* (for future) in the presentation, but do not ask students to produce it until it is formally presented on page 101.

Ask questions like the following to present the pictures.

What is he/she going to do next Tuesday/Wednesday?

Do you think he's/she's going to _____ on Thursday?

Why do you think he/she is(n't) going to _____ on Thursday?

Have/Do you ever _____?

When did you last _____?

How often do you _____?

The following is a sample presentation of story line 1 (Carlos's week).

> Today we're going to talk about what these people are going to do next week. What's Carlos going to do on Tuesday? Is he going to check into a hotel or check into a hospital?...He's going to check into a hospital. When do you check into a hospital?...Yes, when you're sick. Does that mean you're going into or leaving the hospital?...It means you're going into it. What else do we check into?...Yes, we check into a hotel. Now, what's Carlos going to do on Wednesday?...He's going to have an operation. What does that mean?...Right. An operation is when they cut you open. Did anyone here ever have an operation?...You did, Pablo? Here, or in your country?...I see. I know, it's no fun. I had an operation three years ago myself. So, on Tuesday, Carlos is going to...check into the hospital. And on Wednesday he's going to...have an operation. Now, what do you think? Is he going to go to work on Thursday?...You say he isn't going to go, Joycelin? Why not?...Because he'll be resting at home. And you think he's going to go, Theo?...Oh, I see, if it's a small operation.

Grammar Box (page 101 of Student Book)

Refer to the procedure on page viii.

Ask students to call out some leisure activities, and write them down on the chalkboard. Then call on individuals to name one leisure activity they're going to do on Sunday. Ask the rest of the class to report and expand on this information. For example:

    T: Tell me a leisure activity you're going to do on Sunday, Danny.

    D: Play tennis.

    T: What's Danny going to do on Sunday, class?

	Ss:	He's going to play tennis.
	T:	Is he going to have fun?
	Ss:	Yes, he is.

After the class has answered several of your questions, have the students make the questions following this model.

	T:	Tell me a leisure activity you're going to do on Sunday, Dolores.
	D:	Relax.
	Ss:	What's she going to do on Sunday?
	T:	She's going to relax.
		(Point to another leisure activity on the list.)
	Ss:	Is she going to go fishing?
	T:	No, she isn't.

Activity 4

Refer to the procedure on page ix.

Teach students the pronunciation of *going to* in informal speech. Write the first conversation on the chalkboard. Cross out the words *going to* and above them write *gunna*. Explain that this is often the pronunciation of *going to* in spoken English. Have students repeat the sentences using *gunna*. Go through the rest of the conversations, using *gunna* in both questions and answers. Encourage students to practice both ways of pronouncing *going to* as they do the pairwork.

Grammar Box (page 102 of Student Book, top)

Refer to the procedure on page viii.

Ask individuals yes/no questions, and have the class restate the information in affirmative and negative statements. For example:

	T:	Are you going to play soccer this weekend, Hiroko?
	H:	No, I'm not.
	T:	Class?
	Ss:	She isn't going to play soccer this weekend.

Activity 5

Tell students to use the pictures on page 99 to write their sentences.

Grammar Box (page 102 of Student Book, bottom)

Refer to the procedure on page viii.

Write the following time expressions on the chalkboard: *after school today, tomorrow night, next weekend, next month, next summer.* Point to them one by one and have students ask you what you're going to do at that time. Then ask individual students what they're going to do and help them respond appropriately. Remind them about the informal pronunciation of *going to.*

Grammar Box (page 103 of Student Book)

Refer to the procedure on page viii.

Give students verbal cues and have them make sentences about next weekend. For example:

	T:	Clean the house, Thierry.
	Th:	I'm not going to clean the house next weekend.

Activity 7

After students finish the writing task, have them share some of their sentences with the class. For reinforcement of *going to*, refer to the Expansion Activity.

Activity 8

Prepare students for the conversation and the activities on page 103 by asking these questions.

When you're sick, do you go to work?; What do you do?; Who do you call?

Activity 9

Help students recall the health problems in the box by miming them and having students say what's wrong. Have them also offer advice. For example:

T: (miming an ear infection) What's the problem?

Ss: You have an ear infection.

T: What can I do about it, Raúl?

R: Go to the doctor.

Activity 10

After students complete the conversation and practice it with their partners, have several pairs of students perform their dialogues for the class.

Expansion Activity

Give students more practice using *going to* in questions and statements. First, draw a page from your weekly calendar on the chalkboard (it must represent a week in the future) and list your planned activities. For example:

NOVEMBER
4 Monday
doctor's appointment - 11:30
5 Tuesday
pay bills
6 Wednesday
call Mom and Dad
7 Thursday
dinner with Anthony - 6:30
8 Friday
pick up photos
9 Saturday
buy Ben's birthday present
10 Sunday
play cards with Marc and Sally - 4:00

Next, have students make similar weekly calendars for themselves. Ask them to list a different activity for every day of the week. Then tell students they will work in pairs, asking their partners about their plans and writing the information down on another sheet of paper.

Before students start the pairwork, model the task. Choose one student and ask about his or her plans for Monday and Tuesday. For example:

T: What are you going to do on Monday, Sam?

S: I'm going to buy a computer.

T: Are you going to use a credit card?

S: Yes, I am.

T: What are you going to do on Tuesday?

S: I'm going to visit my son's school.

T: Are you going to go with your wife?

S: No, I'm not.

Then write the following sentences on the chalkboard.

On Monday, Sam is going to buy a computer. He's going to use a credit card.

On Tuesday, he's going to visit his son's school. He isn't going to go with his wife.

Tell students to ask their partners about all seven days of the week and to write two sentences about their partners' activities on each day. As students are doing the pairwork, circulate to make sure they're doing the activity correctly. When they've finished writing, collect their papers.

A. **Carlos is going to have an operation on Wednesday morning. Read the doctor's instructions about what he can and cannot do before and after the operation.**

On Tuesday, you can eat regular meals for breakfast and lunch. For dinner, you can eat a light meal of toast and vegetable soup. Do not eat meat. After dinner, you must not eat any food. You can drink water and juice, but do not drink milk or alcohol.

On Wednesday morning, you must not eat or drink anything. Come to the hospital one hour early. First, go to the admitting desk and fill out a form. Then take the elevator to the Surgery Department in the basement.

After the operation, you cannot drive home by yourself. Someone has to drive you home.

B. **These instructions are not in the correct order. Number them correctly.**

_____ First, go to the admitting desk and fill out a form.

_____ After dinner, do not eat any food.

_____ On Wednesday morning, do not eat or drink anything.

___1___ On Tuesday, eat regular meals for breakfast and lunch.

_____ Drink water and juice, but do not drink milk or alcohol.

_____ Do not drive home by yourself.

_____ For dinner, eat toast and vegetable soup, but do not eat meat.

_____ Take the elevator to the Surgery Department in the basement.

_____ Come to the hospital one hour early.

C. **Write sentences about Carlos. Use *going to*.**

1. <u>He's going to eat regular meals for breakfast and lunch on Tuesday.</u>

2. <u>He isn't going to eat meat for dinner.</u>

3. _____

4. _____

5. _____

6. _____

7. _____

8. _____

9. _____

When Is Ken Going to Move?

Topic: housing

Life Skill/Competency: ordering services

Structure: future *going to*

Vocabulary

move to a new apartment   ride a merry-go-round

buy four chairs   walk

take them home   play checkers

see a movie   do nothing

Teaching Suggestions

Activity 1

Refer to the procedure on page v.

This unit is atypical in that students will be producing statements just after you have presented the vocabulary, as in the sample presentation below. Allow several students to produce each of the statements, and allow extra time for this presentation.

A. Ask these questions about Ken on Friday.

1.	What's Ken going to do?	(Move to a new apartment.)
2.	Where's he going to move?	(Around the corner [from his old place].)
3.	What time is he going to move?	(In the morning.)

Ask these questions about Ken on Saturday.

1.	What's Ken going to do on Saturday?	(Buy chairs for his new apartment.)
2.	How many chairs is he going to buy?	(Four.)
3.	Who's he going to go shopping for the chairs with?	(Judy.)
4.	How's he going to take the chairs home?	(In his car.)

B. Ask these questions about the kids on Friday.

1.	What are the kids going to do on Friday?	(See a movie.)
2.	Where are they going to see the movie?	(Downtown.)
3.	Who are they going to go to the movie with?	(Their parents.)
4.	When are they going to see the movie?	(At night.)

Ask these questions about the kids on Saturday.

1.	What are the kids going to do on Saturday?	(Ride a merry-go-round.)
2.	Where are they going to ride the merry-go-round?	(At the park.)
3.	When are they going to go to the park?	(In the afternoon.)
4.	How are they going to get to the park?	([They're going to] walk.)

C. Ask these questions about the cat on Friday.

1. What's the cat going to do on Friday?   (Play checkers.)
2. When's the cat going to play checkers?   (All day.)
3. Who's the cat going to play with?   (The parrot.)
4. Where are they going to play?   (In the living room.)

Ask this question about the cat on Saturday.

What's the cat going to do on Saturday?   (Nothing.)

The following is a sample presentation of Picture 1 (what Ken is going to do on Friday).

> Let's see what Ken's going to do next Friday. Is he going to paint his house, or is he going to move?...He's going to move. What does that mean?...Yes, it means change to a new house. Did any of you move recently?...You did, Kim? Where did you move to?...To Taylor Street. Now, where's Ken going to move to [pointing]?...Yes, he's going to move around the corner from his old apartment. So is he going to move far or close to his old place?...Close. Just around the corner. And when is he going to move [pointing]?...He's going to move in the morning. How do you know?...Yes, because the sun is going up. Now look at the picture and listen. [Slowly, pointing to individual parts of the picture:] On Friday morning, Ken's going to move to a new apartment around the corner. Who can say that?...Joon, you want to try? Go ahead...

Grammar Box (page 107 of Student Book)

Refer to the procedure on page viii.

Use dolls, puppets, or pictures to practice *Wh-* questions with *going to*. (You'll need a male and a female.) Write *what* on the chalkboard and ask students to recall other *Wh-* words they've studied. List them on the board under *what*. Then hold up one of the dolls, puppets, or pictures, point to *what*, and tell students to ask a question about what he or she is going to do next weekend. Point to other *Wh-* words and have individual students ask the corresponding questions. In response to their questions, you'll invent a story. For example:

T: (holding up the female and pointing to *what*)

Ss: What is she going to do?

T: She's going to go shopping.

(pointing to *where*)

Ss: Where is she going to go shopping?

T: At May's Department Store.

(pointing to *when*)

Ss: When is she going to go shopping?

T: On Saturday.

(pointing to *how*)

Ss: How is she going to go shopping?

T: By bus.

(pointing to *who*)

Ss: Who is she going to go shopping with?

T: Her sisters.

After students ask about both the male and the female, hold the two up together so the class can invent a story using *they*.

Activity 3

Refer to the procedure on page ix.

When you practice the conversations with the students, review the pronunciation of *going to* in informal speech. Write the first conversation on the chalkboard. Cross out the words *going to* and above them write *gunna*. Have students repeat the sentences using *gunna*. Go through the rest of the conversations in like manner. Encourage students to practice both ways of pronouncing *going to* during the pairwork.

Grammar Box (page 108 of Student Book)

Refer to the procedure on page viii.

Ask students various *Wh-* questions about activities they're planning to do next weekend and next summer. They may answer with short answers or complete sentences. Then have them ask you about your plans for next weekend and next summer.

Activity 4

When students close their books to do the pairwork, have the following *Wh-* words on the chalkboard: *what, where, what day, what time, who...with, how.*

Ask a few students to talk about their partners before the writing task. After students finish writing, have more of them share sentences about their partners with the class.

For reinforcement of questions with *going to*, refer to Expansion Activity 1.

Activity 5

Refer to the procedure on page x.

To help students recall the services, bring in pictures of a gas stove, an electrical outlet, and a trash can, or draw simple sketches of these objects on the chalkboard. Ask students if they have to pay for these services in their homes. In addition, ask these questions to prepare students for the conversation and the listening task.

When you move to a new apartment, is there a telephone there?; How do you get a telephone?; Who do you call?; What other services do you have to order?; Do you ever have to pay money for a deposit? How much?

Explain that new customers—those who do not already have accounts with the various utility companies—must sometimes pay a small amount of money called a *deposit,* which is returned when they stop the service.

Activity 6

Before students listen to the tape the first time, have them cover up the columns labeled *Deposit* and *Amount* with a piece of paper. Have them uncover these columns for the second listening.

For more practice ordering services, refer to Expansion Activity 2.

Activity 7

As students work with their partners to answer the questions, circulate to explain unfamiliar terms and to show them where to look for answers they can't find. After students have finished the writing task, check their work by having volunteers write the answers on the chalkboard.

For more practice reading utility bills, refer to Expansion Activity 3.

Expansion Activities

1. Give students additional practice making questions and answers with *going to* by playing a modified version of the game "Twenty Questions." First, review question formation by asking students several *Wh-* and yes/no questions about their plans for the weekend and for the summer. Then divide the class into three teams. Put the following cue on the chalkboard: *What are you going to do* _____? Then ask for a volunteer to come to the front of the classroom and answer questions. Have the teams take turns asking this person *Wh-* and yes/no questions about the future, beginning with the question cued on the board. Keep score on the board, awarding one point each time a grammatically correct and meaningful question is asked. After the first student has answered ten questions, have that student sit down and another student take his or her place. The game may continue for as long as it serves as a useful review of the structure. The team with the highest number of points in the end wins the game.

2. Strip Story. Using the dialogue on page 109 of the Student Book as a model, type out a new dialogue about ordering another type of service and cut it into strips of paper, with one strip per line of text. Put students into pairs and give each pair all of the strips necessary to create the dialogue. (The strips should not be in order.) Ask students to arrange the strips to create a conversation. Then have them practice the conversation aloud.

3. Photocopy one or more utility bills and pass out copies to pairs of students in the class. Dictate or write on the chalkboard five or six questions about each bill, using the questions on page 110 as a guide. Have students work with their partners to scan the bills for answers to the questions and write them on a piece of paper. To check for comprehension and accuracy, have volunteers write the answers on the board.

Look at this telephone bill. Write answers to the questions below.

	Lifeline Telephone Company	
Account number	510862-4637N107	
Statement date	Nov. 10, 1996	
Previous bill	35.29	
Payment 10/15 Thank you	35.29	
Balance	.00	
Current charges:		
Lifeline	12.95	
Coast to Coast	13.38	
Current charges due 12/16		**26.33**
Total due		**26.33**
For billing questions call:		
Lifeline	No charge	788-0965
Coast to Coast	No charge	1-800-624-7000
Regular monthly service		
Basic service		12.00
Tax		.95
Total Lifeline monthly service		**12.95**
Coast to Coast long-distance charges		

Item	Date	Time	Min.	Rate	Place	Number	Charge
1	Nov 1	7:35 P	15	E	Portland, OR	503 228-1159	2.97
2	Nov 4	9:06 A	4	D	Seattle, WA	203 464-8602	.60
3	Nov 4	11:10 P	57	N	Chicago, IL	312 787-4470	5.70
4	Nov 7	5:45 P	31	E	Detroit, MI	313 644-8452	4.11
Total long-distance charges							**13.38**

1. What is the name of the telephone company?_____

2. What is the account number?_____

3. How much is the regular monthly service? _____

4. What is the name of the long-distance company? _____

5. How many long-distance calls are there? _____

6. What are the total charges for long-distance calls? _____

7. When is the total payment due? _____

8. What can you do if you have questions about the bill? _____

_____

UNIT 18 | Will I Be Rich?

Topic: predictions

Life Skill/Competency: asking a favor

Structure: future *will*

Vocabulary

be rich	go back to my country
be famous	travel around the world
meet the president	go to the moon
get a raise	have great-grandchildren
get a promotion	have white hair
get a new job	

Teaching Suggestions
Activity 1

Refer to the procedure on page v.

Focus on the vocabulary during the presentation, using any appropriate structures to talk about it. Do not focus on the modal *will* until the questions and responses are formally presented on page 113.

Ask questions like the following to present the pictures.

Do you want to _____?

Why do(n't) you want to _____?

Do you think you will _____?

Why do(n't) you think you will _____?

Do you know people who _____?

The following is a sample presentation of Picture 1 (be rich).

> Today I'm going to ask you some questions about the future. See this guy? He has a lot of...money. That means he's...rich. Now who here wants to be rich in the future?...Everyone does. No surprise. But tell me, Diego, why do you want to be rich?...Oh, so you can buy a new house. And you, Helen, why do you want to be rich?...Oh, to go back to your country. And Kevin, do you think you'll be rich?...You don't? How come?...Because it's hard to find a good job here. I understand. What about you, Teresa, do you think you'll be rich someday?...You do!...Oh, you have a good idea for a business. I wish you good luck!

Grammar Box (page 113 of Student Book)

Refer to the procedure on page viii.

Explain that *will*, like *going to*, is a way of talking about the future. Ask students to volunteer information about things they want to have or do in the future, and make a list of these things on the chalkboard. (The list may include such items as *have a big house*, *visit my brother in Australia*, and *speak English well*.) Then call on students to ask each other yes/no questions. If the response is affirmative, the questioner should ask a second question beginning with *When*. For example:

> T: Marta, ask Khalid a question.
>
> M: Will I get a job I like?
>
> K: Yes, you will.
>
> M: When will I get a job I like?
>
> K: In three years.

Activity 5

After students have finished the writing task, before having them read their questions aloud, review the intonation patterns for yes/no and *Wh-* questions. Write the example sentences on the chalkboard. Model them for the students, and have them say whether your voice goes up or down at the end of each question. Mark the intonation patterns with arrows.

Will I have a big family?

When will I see my sister again?

Ask students to recall why the intonation patterns for the questions are different. Then have them repeat the questions using the correct intonation.

Provide the opportunity for students to share some of their questions with the class and practice their intonation. Ask three students to assume the role of fortune-tellers. Have them come to the front of the room and sit facing the class. Ask each of these students to choose a name (you may suggest names such as *Mr. X* or *Madame Globotzny*). Write these names on notecards and prop them up in front of the fortune-tellers. Then call on members of the class to ask their yes/no and *when* questions, reminding them to use the correct intonation. The fortune-tellers may give any answers they wish.

For reinforcement of yes/no questions and answers with *will*, refer to Expansion Activity 1.

Activity 6

Explain that we often use *will* in sentences that begin with *If*. Before students start the writing task, have individual students make statements about what they will and won't do under some of the conditions mentioned in the exercise. For any given item, call on three students so that the class understands there are many different ways in which to complete each sentence. After students finish writing, have them share some of their sentences with the class.

Activity 7

Before students start the pairwork, model the example question and answer and have the class repeat. Then ask several students these questions.

What will you do if you feel sick tomorrow?; What will you do if it's noisy outside your apartment tonight?; What will you do if you lose your job?; What will you do if you don't understand your homework?

Point out that students must use the simple present form of the verb in their questions with *if*. Their partners' answers, however, must be expressed with *will*. As students write their questions and do the pairwork, circulate to make sure they're doing the activity correctly.

For reinforcement of real conditionals, refer to Expansion Activity 2.

Activity 8

Refer to the procedure on page x.

Prepare students for the activities on pages 115 and 116 by asking these questions.

What do you do if you need an egg for something you're cooking and you don't have it?; What do you do if all the stores are closed?; Do you ever borrow *an egg from your neighbor? From a friend?; What other things do you borrow from friends and members of your family?*

In addition, explain that *do me a favor* means *help me*.

Activity 9

Before students start the listening task, do a quick review of common household objects by saying a number and having the class call out the names of the three items pictured next to that number.

Activity 11

After students have completed the conversations and practiced them with their partners, have several pairs of students perform their dialogues for the class.

Expansion Activities

1. Review yes/no questions and answers with *will* by having students do a mingling activity in which they move around the room asking their classmates questions. Pass out copies of (or have students copy from the chalkboard) the following form.

Find 3 people who will take classes here next year.	Find 3 people who will go back to their countries this summer.
1. _____	1. _____
2. _____	2. _____
3. _____	3. _____
Find 3 people who will attend college in the United States.	Find 3 people who will go out of town this weekend.
1. _____	1. _____
2. _____	2. _____
3. _____	3. _____

Before starting the activity, read the instructions with the students and explain unfamiliar vocabulary. Then write the following cues on the board—*Will you...? Yes, I will. No, I won't.*—and model the task. Circulate and ask several students if they will take classes next year. Write the names of those who answer in the affirmative on your form. Help students recall the correct intonation for yes/no questions (rising) and short answers (rising/falling) and encourage them to use the correct intonation as they ask and answer questions. Then erase the board and have all students stand up and begin interviewing their classmates.

2. Give students additional practice with real conditionals by dictating these partial sentences and having students complete them.

   If I get a promotion,

   If I get a sore throat,

   If it's rainy tomorrow,

   If I find cockroaches in the house,

   If I lose my wallet,

   If I go back to my country,

   If I meet the president,

   If I buy a car,

   If I learn another language,

   If I come to school next year,

   You may have students share their sentences with the class and/or hand them in.

A. **Read Judy's letter to her friend Debbie.**

Dear Debbie,   March 13
     How are you? I'm fine. Everybody here at the bicycle factory is well
again, and we're all back to work.
     We're having a party for the factory employees a week from Sunday.
It's a little hard to plan, though. We don't know what the weather will be like.
     If it's sunny, we'll have a picnic at Blair Park. We'll find a nice place
under a tree. We'll cook hamburgers and hot dogs on a grill, and we'll eat
on picnic tables. If it's rainy, we won't have a picnic. We'll have a party at
Susan's house **instead**. Everyone will bring some food. We'll put all the food
on Susan's dining room table. Everyone will serve themselves. If it's sunny,
we'll want a lot of cold drinks, like soda and juice. If it's rainy, we'll probably
serve hot drinks, like coffee and tea. If it's sunny, we'll play outdoor games,
like soccer and volleyball. If it's rainy, we'll play indoor games. Susan has a
Ping-Pong table in her basement, and we'll set up card tables so people can
play cards. Either way, we'll have a lot of fun.
     We can bring our friends to the party. If you're going to be in town that
Sunday, why don't you come to the party with me? Let me know if you can.
                                                                              Love,
                                                                              Judy

B. **Write what will happen if it's sunny and if it's rainy.**

If it's sunny	If it's rainy
They'll have a picnic at Blair Park.	They won't have a picnic.

What Did Carlos Do on Monday?

Topic: banking

Life Skill/Competency: opening a bank account

Structure: past tense

Vocabulary

open a bank account	gamble all day
deposit money	return the money
shop all day	look at mice
close the bank account	chase mice
borrow money	cook the mice
travel to Las Vegas	do nothing

checking account   savings account   service charge   interest

Teaching Suggestions

Activity 1

Refer to the procedure on page v.

Use the past tense in your presentation, but do not ask students to produce it until it is formally introduced on page 119.

Ask questions like the following to present the pictures.

What did (Carlos) do on (Tuesday)?

Why did (he) _____? (free speculation)

Do/Did you ever _____?

How much (money) did you _____?

When did you _____?

Does your cat ever _____?

The following is a sample presentation for Picture 1 (open a bank account).

> Today we're going to talk about what these people did last week. What did Carlos do on Monday?...Well, did he open a book, or open a bank account?...He opened a bank account. What is a bank account?...Yes, it's when we keep our money in the bank. And what does it mean to open an account?...Yes, it means we start a new account. Did any of you open an account when you came here?...You did, Heng Li? When did you open your account?...Last year. Where?...At First National. Now, why do you think Carlos opened a new account?...Yes, maybe he just moved. Or?...Oh, Chen, what an idea! You think he wants to hide his money from his wife! Well, could be...

Grammar Box (page 119 of Student Book, top)

Refer to the procedure on page viii.

Write *last night* and *yesterday* on the chalkboard. Ask students what other past time expressions they know of and write these on the board too. In addition, put the following list of regular verbs on the board.

study	fix	clean	wash	visit
play	talk	watch	shop	relax
work	travel	repair	call	move

Point to the different time expressions and have students make sentences about themselves using the past tense of these regular verbs. Keep this list on the board for use with the next grammar box.

Activity 4

After students have repeated the verbs in the box after you, ask them to figure out the rule for the pronunciation of long and short endings on verbs in the past tense. After students have circled *S* or *L* in the exercise, check for accuracy by saying the number of an item and having students call out *short sound* or *long sound*. Any items that students have trouble with may be clarified as follows. Write both the simple form and the past-tense form of the verb on the board. As you model each form, clap out the syllables and have students tell you how many syllables it has. (Only when the verb ends in the sound /t/ or /d/ will the past-tense form have an additional syllable.) For more practice, have students go through this list of verbs again, clapping out the syllables and then pronouncing the past-tense form of the verbs.

Grammar Box (page 119 of Student Book, middle)

Refer to the procedure on page viii.

Tell students they're going to talk about what happened last week. Supply time cues and have individuals make statements about themselves using the regular verbs from the list already on the board. Then have half of the class ask a third-person question and the other half give the answer. For example:

> T: On Monday, Vinh.
>
> V: On Monday, I washed my clothes.
>
> Ss1: What did he do on Monday?
>
> Ss2: He washed his clothes.

Activity 6

If students need additional practice spelling the past-tense form of verbs, put these verbs on the board and tell students to add *-ed*. Explain the meanings of any verbs students aren't familiar with.

ask	continue	jog	hurry	pray
park	study	borrow	hop	use
skip	travel	hope	enjoy	listen

Activity 7

Before students start the writing task, read aloud the verbs in the box and have students repeat. Ask several students to make sentences aloud about things they did within the past month. Then have them write. After they finish, have them share some of their sentences with the class.

For reinforcement of regular verbs in the past tense, refer to Expansion Activity 1.

Activity 8

Refer to the procedure on page x.

Introduce the new vocabulary and prepare students for the activities on pages 121 and 122 by asking these questions.

> *Do you have a bank account?; Is it a* checking *account or a* savings *account?; Do you have a* checkbook? *Can you show us your checkbook?; Is there a* service charge *on your checking account? How much is it?; Who pays the service charge—do you pay the bank or does the bank pay you?; Is there* interest *on your savings account? How much is it?; Who pays the interest—do you pay the bank or does the bank pay you?; Who do you talk to when you go to the bank?*

Activity 9

Have students read the three possible answers aloud before listening to each question on the tape. Stop the tape between each item in the exercise.

Activity 10

As you read about the different checking and savings accounts with the students, ask several students if their bank accounts require a minimum balance and, if so, what the amount is.

Activity 11

After the students have completed the conversation and practiced it with their partners, have several pairs of students perform their dialogues for the class.

Activity 12

After students have written answers to the questions, have four students write their sentences on the chalkboard and read them aloud to the class. Point out that the first two answers are in the past tense and the last two are in the future and require the use of *will*.

For reinforcement of language related to banking, refer to Expansion Activity 2.

Expansion Activities

1. Write *Last Sunday* on the chalkboard and dictate the following short paragraph for students to write.

    Last Sunday, Susan stayed home with her family. In the morning, she cooked a big breakfast. After the meal, she washed the dishes. Next, she typed a letter to her mother. In the afternoon, she cleaned the kitchen and the bathroom. Later, she played cards with Linda. Sunday night, Susan relaxed with the family. They watched TV all evening.

    Check for comprehension and accuracy by having volunteers write the eight sentences on the chalkboard. Then have students write a short paragraph about their own activities the previous Sunday. To ensure that students don't use irregular verbs, you may put a list of familiar regular verbs on the board (see the Teaching Suggestions for the grammar box found at the top of page 119 of the Student Book and the box of verbs for Activity 7 on page 120 of the Student Book) and suggest that students choose verbs from this list.

2. Photocopy brochures from local banks listing various types of checking and savings accounts. Give one copy of the brochures to each pair of students in the class. Write questions similar to the following on the chalkboard.

    What is the name of the bank?; How many accounts are there?; How many are checking accounts, and how many are savings accounts?; Is there a service charge on the checking accounts? How much is it?; Is there a minimum balance on the checking accounts? How much is it?; Do any of the checking accounts earn interest? How much?; Is there a minimum balance on the savings accounts? How much is it?; How much interest do the savings accounts earn?

    Have students work with their partners to write answers to the questions. When they've finished, have them write the information on the board.

A. **Read about the Satos' daughter, Kathy.**

Last week was a very busy week for Kathy. On Sunday afternoon, she graduated from college in San Diego. On Monday, she moved back to Los Angeles. She stayed in her parents' apartment on Monday night. On Tuesday morning, she looked for a place to live. She rented a small furnished apartment that afternoon. On Wednesday morning, Kathy looked for a job in the Help Wanted ads. She called several companies. That afternoon, she talked with Mr. Gifford, the owner of a small computer company. Thursday morning, Kathy started work at the Gifford Computer Company. She worked all day on Thursday and Friday. Friday night, she visited her cousins' house for dinner. On Saturday morning, Kathy opened a new bank account and deposited $3,000. Then she shopped for new clothes all afternoon. When Kathy returned to her apartment at 7:00, she was very, very tired. So she closed her eyes and opened them at 9:00 the next morning!

B. **Read the time words and write questions and answers.**

1. last Sunday

   <u>What did Kathy do last Sunday?</u>

   <u>She graduated from college.</u>

2. on Monday

   _____

   _____

3. Tuesday afternoon

   _____

   _____

4. Wednesday morning

   _____

   _____

5. Thursday morning

   _____

   _____

6. Friday night

   _____

   _____

7. Saturday morning

   _____

   _____

8. Saturday afternoon

   _____

   _____

 **Did You Live Near a Post Office in Your Country?**

Topic: past activities

Life Skill/Competency: postal services

Structure: past tense

Vocabulary

live near a post office	visit museums	attend concerts
pray at church/temple	shop at department stores	live in a big city
watch movies	play sports	travel a lot
use the library	use trains	study English
parcel magazine	large envelope	perishable item

Teaching Suggestions
Activity 1

Refer to the procedure on page v.

Elicit short answers during the presentation, and, if necessary, help students with the responses *Yes, I did* and *No, I didn't.*

Ask questions like the following to present the pictures.

Did you _____ in your country?

How often did you _____?

What kind of _____ did you _____?

Who did you _____ with?

Where did you _____?

Why didn't you _____?

The following is a sample presentation of Pictures 1 and 2 (live near a post office; attend church/temple).

> Today I'm going to ask you about things you did in your country. Ping, did you live near a post office in China?…You did. How far was it?…Oh, across the street. That is close! Did you live near a post office in Burma, Mei Lin?…You didn't. And you, Francisco?…You didn't, either. Now, let's look at the next picture. What's this?…It's a church. What do people do at church [demonstrating with hands]?…People pray. Are there many temples in China, Kim?…There are? And in Vietnam?…Yes. What about in Guatemala?…Oh, mostly churches there. Did you pray at church in Guatemala, Juan?…You did. Who did you go to church with?…Your family. What about you, Mei Lin? Did you pray at temples in Burma?…You did. How often did you pray?…Every day. When do people usually pray in this country?…Yes, often on Sundays.

Grammar Box (page 125 of Student Book, top)

Refer to the procedure on page viii.

Have students brainstorm for a list of daily and weekly household chores, such as *take a shower, wash the dishes, do the laundry,* and write these on the chalkboard. (Leave this list on the board for use with the next grammar box.) Ask a few students if they did one of these activities *yesterday.* Write two of these questions and answers on the chalkboard and ask students to recall the intonation patterns for yes/no questions and short answers. Mark the intonation with arrows.

Did you brush your teeth yesterday?

Yes, I did.

Did you take out the garbage yesterday?

No, I didn't.

Have students repeat the questions and answers using the correct intonation. Then call on individuals to ask and answer questions about activities they may or may not have done the day before. For example:

> T: Alba, ask José a question.
>
> A: Did you sweep the floor yesterday?
>
> J: No, I didn't.

Help students with intonation as they make their questions and answers.

Activity 4

After you practice the first conversation with the students, write *How often?* on the chalkboard. Have students generate a list of familiar expressions of frequency, such as *a lot, every Sunday, once in a while, every two weeks, not very much,* and write these expressions on the board. Students may need to refer to this list when they start the pairwork. After the pairwork is well underway, erase the list from the board.

Grammar Box (page 125 of Student Book, middle)

Refer to the procedure on page viii.

Use the list of daily and weekly household chores on the chalkboard to give students practice making affirmative and negative statements about their activities *yesterday*. One by one, point to the activities on the list and have different students make statements about themselves. Point out that we use the simple form of the verb after *didn't*. In addition, help students pronounce the past-tense form of the verbs correctly using the long or short ending in affirmative sentences.

Activity 5

Before students start the writing task, have them turn back to page 123 and make statements about what they did and didn't do in their native countries. After they finish writing, have them share some of their sentences with the class.

For reinforcement of yes/no questions and statements in the past tense, refer to Expansion Activity 1.

Activity 6

If possible, have realia on hand to reinforce the following vocabulary items: *letter, parcel, magazine,* and *large envelope*. Explain the expression *perishable item* by asking students what foods need to be kept in the refrigerator and listing a few, such as *meat, fish,* and *eggs,* on the chalkboard. As you discuss the four vocabulary items, ask students if they've received or sent these things and, if so, what was inside.

Activity 7

Prepare students for this activity and subsequent activities on pages 126 and 127 by asking these questions.

> *What happens when the mail carrier tries to deliver a parcel and you're not home?; What color*
>
> *is the notice?; Where does the mail carrier leave it?; What can you do if you receive a notice?*

As you read through the notice with the students, take time to explain the various options for obtaining a piece of mail, which are listed on the left side of the notice.

Activities 11 and 12

After checking students' answers to the questions, call their attention to the notes in the box.

For reinforcement of language related to postal services, refer to Expansion Activities 2 and 3.

Expansion Activities

1. Review yes/no questions in the past tense by questioning a few students about things they may or may not have done in their countries, using vocabulary from the first page of the unit. Then draw this chart on the chalkboard and have students copy it.

Classmates' names:			
wash clothes by hand			
cook on a wood stove			
live in a big house			
use computers			
watch TV			
travel by car			

Go over the verb phrases with the class, explaining any unfamiliar vocabulary. Then tell students to interview three of their classmates. Students should write the name of each classmate they interview at the top of a column, ask each classmate six yes/no questions, and fill in the chart with *yes* or *no*. Remind students to use the correct intonation in their questions and answers. Then have students write short paragraphs about what each of their three classmates did and didn't do in their countries.

2. Bring in a parcel, a magazine, a large envelope, a package labeled "perishable" and some yellow postal notices (which you have filled out before class). Use these items in role-plays. First, practice the dialogue on page 127 with the students. Then have the class improvise a dialogue in which the mail item is available to be picked up. Next, put the postal items on a table in the corner and pass out the postal notices. Ask volunteers to come to the front of the classroom and role-play dialogues between a postal clerk and a customer. (When the customer presents the postal notice to the clerk, the clerk may either "find" the item that the customer requests or say when the customer can return for it.)

3. Pass out change of address forms to all students in the class. Remind them that they may use this form to notify the post office of a temporary change of address, which may occur when they go on vacation, or any permanent change of address that they anticipate. Show them where to print their names and old addresses and where to sign their names. If some students are about to go on vacation or move, help them fill out the rest of the form. Urge students to keep the change of address form on hand until they need it.

A. Read the letter from Linda's grandmother.

Dear Linda,   March 28
    How are you? I'm fine. I liked your last letter very much.
    You asked about the past. What did I do when I was eight years old?
Well, life was different back then. I lived in a very small town. I studied in a
one-room school building from 8:00 in the morning to 3:00 in the afternoon.
After school, I helped my mother. We cooked and cleaned the house.
Sometimes I played outside with my brother. But we didn't have any toys!
    We didn't travel very much back then. Of course, we didn't have a car.
When we visited relatives, we used the train. There were no TVs back then.
There was no movie theater in my town. When we wanted to have a good
time, we attended church **socials**. As for shopping, there were no department
stores back then. If I needed a new dress, my mother sewed it for me.
    That's how life was when I was a girl! Write soon and tell me more
about your life right now.
                                                    Love,
                                                    Grandma

**B. Read the questions about Linda's grandmother when she was a girl. Write
     short answers.**

1. Did Linda's grandmother live in a small town?   <u>**Yes, she did.**</u>

2. Did she go to a big school?   _____

3. Did she help her mother after school?   _____

4. Did her parents have a lot of money?   _____

5. Did they have a car?   _____

6. Did Linda's grandmother travel by train?   _____

7. Did she watch movies?   _____

8. Did she attend church?   _____

9. Did she shop at department stores?   _____

10. Did her mother buy her new clothes?   _____

 **Did You Go Shopping Last Weekend?**

Topic: weekend activities

Life Skill/Competency: returning/exchanging clothing

Structure: past tense

Vocabulary

go shopping	have fun	leave the city
see friends	come home late	write a letter
eat out	meet somebody new	speak English
get a haircut	sleep late	tell a lie

Teaching Suggestions
Activity 1

Refer to the procedure on page v.

Ask questions like the following to present the pictures.

Did you _____ last weekend?

Where did you _____?

Who did you _____ with?

How did you get there?

When was the last time you _____?

Why didn't you _____?

The following is a sample presentation of Picture 1 (go shopping).

> Today we're going to talk about things we did last weekend. Noe, did you go shopping last weekend?...You didn't. What about you, Silvia, did you go shopping last weekend?...Yes, you did. And where did you go shopping?...In Chinatown. Who did you go with?...Your mother. And you, Mohammed? Did you go shopping?...You did. How did you get to the store?...You drove. OK, let's go to the next picture. Jin Tong, did you see your friends last weekend?...

Activity 3

Refer to the procedure on page ix.

As you practice the conversations with the students, help them produce the questions and short answers using the correct intonation. Remind them to use correct intonation during the pairwork.

Grammar Box (page 131 of Student Book, top)

Refer to the procedure on page viii.

Write on the chalkboard the present- and past-tense forms of three regular verbs such as *wait, kiss,* and *brush.* Then write the present- and past-tense forms of three irregular verbs such as *go, do,* and *have.* Explain that while the past tense of regular verbs is formed by adding *-ed,* the past-tense forms of irregular verbs do not follow this pattern and must be learned individually.

Activity 4

As you introduce each new irregular verb, use it in a sentence about yourself and ask two students to make sentences following your model. For example:

> T: I came to school at 8:00 this morning. What about you, Wipula?
>
> W: I came to school at 9:45.
>
> T: And you, Maribel?
>
> M: I came to school at 10:00.

Grammar Box (page 131 of Student Book, middle)

Refer to the procedure on page viii.

Remind students that the simple form of the verb, and not the past-tense form, follows *didn't*. Supply cues from among the irregular verbs and have students make affirmative and negative statements about *yesterday*. For example:

> T: Eat chicken, Salah.
>
> S: I ate chicken yesterday.
>
> T: Go to the bank, Xiaoping.
>
> X: I didn't go to the bank yesterday.

Activity 5

After students finish the writing task, have them share some of their sentences with the class.

Activity 6

Before students start this task, make eight columns on the chalkboard and write at the top of the columns the simple and past-tense forms of the verbs. Then, as you model the pronunciation of each verb, have students brainstorm for one complement, and write that complement in the appropriate column. Then put students in groups of three or four and have them work to complete their lists with the members of their group. When the lists are finished, have the different groups share the items on their lists with the class, and write all items in the appropriate columns on the chalkboard.

Prepare students for the writing task by pointing to a couple of items on these lists and making statements about yourself, and then having students make sentences about themselves. For example:

> T: (pointing to *wear pants*) I wore pants to school yesterday.
>
> (pointing to *ride a horse*) I didn't ride a horse last summer.
>
> (pointing to *drink coffee*) Myrtis.
>
> M: I drank coffee this morning.
>
> T: (pointing to *feel well*) Stephanie.
>
> S: I didn't feel well last night.

After students finish the writing task, have them share some of their sentences with the class.

For reinforcement of irregular past-tense verbs, refer to Expansion Activity 1.

Activity 7

Refer to the procedure on page x.

Prepare students for the activities on pages 133 and 134 by asking these questions.

> *What do you do if you buy something and it's too big or too small?; Can you always return it?; Do you sometimes return things? Why?; Can you return things in your country?; Can you always exchange things?; Do you sometimes exchange things? Why?; Can you exchange things in your country?*

After you practice the conversations with the students, do a mini-lesson on intonation in choice questions and responses. Write the following sentences from the dialogue on the chalkboard, model them, and ask students to listen for when your voice goes up and down. Mark the intonation with arrows, as follows.

Do you want to return it or exchange it for a large?

I'd like to exchange it, please.

Have students repeat the question and answer using the correct intonation. Then write the following question and answer on the chalkboard, and have students tell you how to mark the proper intonation.

Do you want the dress or the blouse?

I'd like the blouse, please.

Explain that when we offer someone a choice of two items, our voice goes up on the first item and down on the second item. When we answer, our voice goes down on the item we select, and starts low and goes up on the word *please*. Have students repeat this question and answer using the correct intonation. Then have students brainstorm for a list of clothes that could be purchased at a department store, and write this list on the board. Call on pairs of students to make and respond to choice questions using items from the list. Help them use the correct intonation.

Activity 10

After students have made new conversations with their partners, call on several pairs of students to perform their dialogues for the class.

For more practice with returns and exchanges, refer to Expansion Activity 2.

Expansion Activities

1. Write the following words on the chalkboard—*wonderful, presents, merry-go-round, root beer*—and explain what they mean if students don't already know. Then dictate the following short paragraph for students to write.

   On Paul's last birthday, he had a wonderful time. When he got out of bed, he went to the living room. Ten presents were waiting for him there! He opened all the presents. He was very happy. Then he went to the park with his family. He rode the merry-go-round. He ate cake and ice cream. He drank root beer. His father bought him a T-shirt. He came home late that night. He cried because he didn't want his birthday to end!

   Check for comprehension and accuracy by having volunteers write the sentences on the board. Then write the phrase *On my last birthday* on the board and have students write a short paragraph about what they did to celebrate their last birthday. Encourage them to use the irregular verbs presented on pages 131 and 132.

2. Strip Story. Using the dialogues on pages 133 and 134 of the Student Book as models, type out a new dialogue and cut it into strips of paper, with one strip per line of text. Put students into pairs and give each pair all of the strips necessary to create the dialogue. (The strips should not be in order.) Ask students to arrange the strips to create a conversation. Then have them practice the conversation aloud.

A.   **Read about Ken and Judy's shopping trip last Saturday.**

On Saturday morning, Ken and Judy went shopping downtown. They bought a lot of things. They got flowers for Ken's mother and a pair of gloves for his brother. For Judy's parents, they bought some plants. They bought hats for Judy's sisters and a watch for her brother. Judy also bought a dress.

When they got home, they took everything out of their shopping bags. They liked some things a lot, but they weren't sure they liked everything. So they went back downtown Saturday afternoon. They exchanged the gloves for a pair of pants. They also bought some socks for Ken's father. They returned the hats. And finally, Judy exchanged her dress for a blouse.

B.   **Look at the pictures. Did Ken and Judy keep these things? Write *yes* or *no*.**

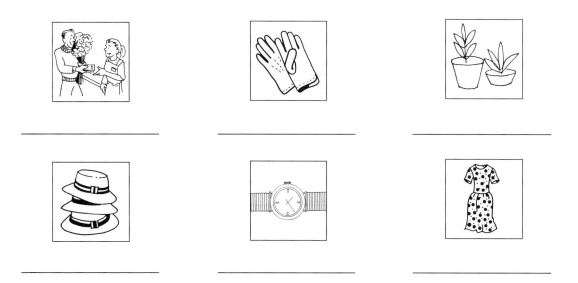

C.   **Write sentences about Ken and Judy's shopping trip. Use *bought* and *got*.**

1.   <u>They bought flowers for Ken's mother.</u>

2.   _____

3.   _____

4.   _____

5.   _____

6.   _____

 **What Happened to Judy?**

Topic: accidents and emergencies

Life Skill/Competency: calling Emergency 911

Structure: past tense

Vocabulary
A dog bit her. Her hand is bleeding.
A car hit him. He's unconscious.
She fell down. She cut her head
She got an electric shock.
He's choking. He can't breathe.
ambulance   emergency room

He drank medicine/poison.
She's having chest pains.
He burned his hand.
He stepped on a nail.

fire truck   police car

Teaching Suggestions
Activity 1

Refer to the procedure on page v.

Look at pages 136 and 137 while presenting page 135. As students look at each picture, ask these questions.

What happened to this person?

What should somebody do to help?

The sentences on pages 136 and 137 comprise the target vocabulary for the presentation (i.e., answers to the above two questions), but students should be encouraged to suggest other ways to describe (or respond to) the problem.

The following is a sample presentation of Picture 1 (a dog bite).

> Today we're going to talk about accidents and emergencies. What are accidents?...Yes, like a car accident. What else?...Yes, when someone falls down. We see several accidents in these pictures. And what's an emergency?...Yes, something very bad—a big problem. And we need...? Yes, we need help fast. Look at the first picture. What happened to Judy?...Yes, a dog bit her. Bit is the past tense of bite. And what does bite mean? Show me...Right, that's what bite is. So this dog bit Judy, and what's happening to her hand?...Yes, it's bleeding. Can you see [pointing to blood]? When you're bleeding, what color is it?...Yes, it's red. Which hand of Judy's is bleeding?...Her right hand. So now that a dog bit Judy and her hand is bleeding, what should we do?...Yes, we can call 911. What else should we do?...Yes, we should wash her hand...What else?...That's called a bandage, Minh. We should put a bandage on her hand. Do you know what a bandage is? Here, let me draw one on the chalkboard for you. Where do you buy bandages?...At the drugstore. Do you keep bandages in your house?...Where?...You keep bandages in the bathroom. Me too. So, we'll wash her hand, put on a bandage, and call 911. Anything else? What about the dog? Is it OK if the dog goes away?...No. How come?...Yes, it can make Judy very sick. So what should we do?...Yes, we should watch the dog until the police come.

Activity 2

Refer to the procedure on page vi.

Use accidents and emergencies to work with students on stress and intonation. First, write the emergency situations on the chalkboard. Then model them one by one. Have students tell you which words are stressed and whether your voice goes up or down at the end of each sentence. Mark the stressed syllables with a dot and the intonation as follows.

A dog bit her. Her hand is bleeding.
A car hit him. He's unconscious.
She fell down. She cut her head.

Explain to students that stressed syllables are louder, higher in pitch, and longer than unstressed syllables. Help students say the sentences quickly and with the proper stress and intonation, clapping on the stressed syllables. Remind students to use correct stress and intonation during the pairwork.

Activity 4

After students finish the listening task, give them additional practice with the vocabulary by miming the different emergencies and asking students what should be done. For example:

T: (miming chest pains) What's happening?

Ss: You're having chest pains.

T: What should I do?

S1: Sit down.

S2: Call the doctor!

T: (miming a car accident and being knocked unconscious) What happened?

Ss: A car hit you.

T: What should someone do?

Ss: Call 911.

Activity 6

Refer to the procedure on page x.

When you introduce the expression *emergency room*, ask students if any of them have ever been to an emergency room in the United States or in their countries. If so, ask them why they were there, what they saw, and how the medical emergency was handled.

Activity 7

Before students listen to the conversations, have them look at the pictures and describe what is happening or what has happened in each one.

Activity 8

After students have read about emergency phone calls and asked any questions they might have, write the following cues on the chalkboard.

A: 911 Emergency.

B: Hello. I need help. _____.

A: _____.

Call on several pairs of students to do short role-plays using the vocabulary in the box.

Activity 10

After students have completed the conversation and practiced it with their partners, have two pairs of students perform their dialogues for the class.

Activity 11

Before students start the writing task, ask them to recall the past-tense form of the verbs in the box.

Activity 12

After students have completed the conversation and practiced it with their partners, have several pairs of students perform their dialogues for the class.

For reinforcement of language related to medical emergencies, refer to Expansion Activities 1, 2, and 3.

Expansion Activities

1. To give students practice responding to medical emergencies, play the "Fly Swatter Game." (You'll need to bring in two fly swatters for the game.) If you have a lot of chalkboard space in your classroom, write the various responses to emergency situations (*Put a bandage on her hand, Let him cough, Wash the cut well, Don't move him*) at different places on the board, and draw a circle around each command. If you don't have much board space, write the various responses on sheets of paper (before class) and tape them to the walls around the classroom. Review the responses by pointing to them and having students read them aloud. Next, divide the class into two teams.

   Now demonstrate how to play the game. With a fly swatter in hand, describe an accident and ask for advice, such as *Paul stepped on a nail! What should we do?* After a student calls out an appropriate response, such as *Wash the cut well,* run to the chalkboard and "swat" the answer with your fly swatter. Next, have two students (from different teams) model the task. Give both students a fly swatter. Tell them to listen for your description of an emergency and "swat" an appropriate response. Then describe an emergency situation. The student who first swats an appropriate response wins a point for his or her team.

   Call on two more students (from different teams) to start the game. Continue playing until all of the students on each team have had a chance to compete. Keep score on the board. The team with the most points wins the game.

2. Give students more practice with language for describing and responding to medical emergencies by having them do role-plays in which they stage an emergency and respond to it. First, put the following skeletal dialogue (modeled on the dialogues on page 138 of the Student Book) on the chalkboard.

   A: Quick! _____!
   B: What _____?
   A: _____.
   B: What should _____?
   A: Let's _____.
   B: OK. I'll _____.

   Review the vocabulary for medical emergencies by taking the part of Speaker A and engaging the class in dialogues about all of the accidents and emergencies introduced on page 135. Then put students in groups of four and hand each group a notecard (which you have made before class) with a description of one of the medical emergencies. Tell group members that they will work together to stage the emergency and respond to it using the cues on the board. Give them ten minutes to plan their role-plays and practice their dialogues. As they're doing this, visit the different groups and give them any coaching they may need. Then erase the cues from the board. Have the various groups come forward to act out their scenarios.

3. For a challenging expansion on the vocabulary presented in Units 21 and 22, ask students to write a short paragraph on a medical emergency that happened to them or to a family member or friend. As they write their stories, circulate to help them with unfamiliar vocabulary and the past tense of unfamiliar irregular verbs. When they finish, have several share their stories with the class. You may also collect their papers.

Read the accident report from the newspaper. Then write answers to the questions. Write complete sentences.

Fire Damages Ace Bicycle Factory

Los Angeles—Fire fighters **raced** to put out a fire at the Ace Bicycle Factory on the corner of 12th and Pike Street yesterday.

Factory owner Gary Sato **reported** the fire at 1:05 p.m. Five minutes later, two fire trucks **arrived** on the scene. Fire fighters worked for 10 minutes to put out the fire in the company stock room.

No one at the bicycle factory was badly hurt. But stock clerk Ken Wong burned his hands trying to put out the fire before fire fighters arrived.

Factory employees aren't sure how the fire started. But when it started, the door to the stock room was open onto the street. Wong **believes** the fire started because of a burning cigarette.

The fire **caused** $500,000 in **damages.**

---

1.   What happened at the Ace Bicycle Factory yesterday?

_____

2.   What time did fire fighters arrive at the factory?

_____

3.   How long did they work to put out the fire?

_____

4.   What room was the fire in?

_____

5.   What happened to Ken Wong?

_____

6.   How did the fire start?

_____

7.   How much damage did the fire cause?

_____

Where Did Carlos Have His Checkup?

Topic: health matters

Life Skill/Competency: medical checkup

Structure: past tense

Vocabulary On Friday, Carlos had a checkup at the clinic at noon. He got there by bus.

On Saturday, he went jogging in the park in the morning. He ran five miles.

On Friday, Judy played tennis with Ken after work. They walked to the playground.

On Saturday, she watched TV at home with her dog because her feet were sore.

On Friday, the parrot talked all day to the cat. He spoke three languages.

On Saturday, he drank lemon and honey tea because he had a sore throat.

He drank seven cups.

heart	kidneys	liver	urinate	congested
lungs	intestine	breathe	nauseous	

Teaching Suggestions
Activity 1

Refer to the procedure on page v.

This unit is atypical in that students will be producing statements just after you have presented the vocabulary, as in the sample presentation below. Allow several students to produce each of the statements and allow extra time for this presentation.

A. Ask these questions about Carlos on Friday:

1. What did Carlos do on Friday?   (He had a checkup.)
2. Where did he have the checkup?   (At the clinic.)
3. When did he have the checkup?   (At noon.)
4. How did he get to the clinic?   (By bus.)

Ask these questions about Carlos on Saturday:

1. What did Carlos do on Saturday?   (He went jogging.)
2. Where did he go jogging?   (In the park.)
3. When did he go jogging?   (In the morning.)
4. How far did he run?   (Five miles.)

B. Ask these questions about Judy on Friday:

1. What did Judy do on Friday?   (She played tennis.)
2. Who did she play tennis with?   (With Ken.)
3. When did they play tennis?   (After work.)
4. How did they get to the park?   (They walked.)

Ask these questions about Judy on Saturday:

1. What did Judy do on Saturday?   (She watched TV.)
2. Where did she watch TV?   (At home.)
3. Who did she watch TV with?   (Her dog.)
4. Why did she watch TV?   (Because her feet were sore.)

C. Ask these questions about the parrot on Friday:

   1. What did the parrot do on Friday?   (He talked all day.)
   2. Who did he talk to?   (The cat.)
   3. How many languages did he speak?   (Three.)

   Ask these questions about the parrot on Saturday:

   1. What did the parrot do on Saturday?   (He drank tea.)
   2. What kind of tea did he drink?   (Lemon and honey tea.)
   3. How many cups did he drink?   (Seven.)
   4. Why did he drink so much tea?   (Because he had a sore throat.)

The following is a sample presentation of Picture 1 (Carlos having a checkup).

> Today we're going to talk about what these people did last Friday and Saturday. What did Carlos do on Friday?...Yes, he had a checkup. What's a checkup?...Yes, when we see the doctor. Because we're sick?...No. We have a checkup to make sure everything's OK. Does Carlos's doctor look happy?...No, he doesn't. Why not, do you think?...Yes, Carlos is too fat. What do you think the doctor told Carlos?...Yes, maybe to get some exercise. Now, where did Carlos go for his checkup [pointing]?...He went to the clinic. Do you remember what a clinic is?...Yes, a doctor's office. When did Carlos have his checkup [pointing]?...At noon. And how did he get to the clinic [pointing]?...He took the bus.

Activity 2

Refer to the procedure on page vi.

Practice the alternation of stressed and unstressed syllables in the target sentences. Write each sentence on the chalkboard. As you model each one, have students tell you which words are stressed. Mark the stressed syllables with dots.

On Friday, Carlos had a checkup at the clinic at noon. He got there by bus.

On Saturday, he went jogging in the park in the morning. He ran five miles.

Remind students that stressed syllables are louder, higher in pitch, and longer than unstressed syllables. Model the sentences again, clapping on the stressed syllables. Have students repeat after you, also clapping on the stressed syllables. Remind students to use correct rhythm and stress during the pairwork.

Grammar Box (page 145 of Student Book)

Refer to the procedure on page viii.

Bring in dolls, puppets, or pictures to practice *Wh-* questions in the past tense. (You'll need a male and a female.) Write *what* on the chalkboard and ask students to recall the other *Wh-* words they've studied. List them on the board under *what*. Then, holding up one of the dolls, puppets, or pictures, point to the *Wh-* words one by one and have students ask questions about last Friday. In response to their questions, you'll invent a story. For example:

   T: (holding up the male and pointing to *what*)
   Ss: What did he do on Friday?
   T: He went to the hospital.
        (pointing to *why*)
   Ss: Why did he go to the hospital?
   T: To visit his father.
        (pointing to *who...with*)

Ss:	Who did he go with?
T:	He went with his wife.
	(pointing to *how*)
Ss:	How did he get there?
T:	By car.
	(pointing to *how long*)
Ss:	How long did he stay there?
T:	An hour and a half.

Have students ask several questions about the male and the female.

Grammar Box (page 146 of Student Book)

Refer to the procedure on page viii.

Ask students various *Wh-* questions about activities they did last weekend and last summer. They may answer with short answers or with complete sentences. Help them if necessary with irregular verb forms. Then point to the *Wh-* words on the board and have students ask you a series of questions about what you did last weekend and last summer.

Activity 4

As students do the pairwork, circulate and help them with any irregular verb forms that may come up. Teach the class those verbs that occur commonly, but avoid overloading students with too many irregular past-tense verbs.

Before students start the writing activity, have a few of them make sentences about their partners aloud. After students finish writing, have them share some of their sentences with the class.

For reinforcement of *Wh-* questions in the past tense, refer to the Expansion Activity.

Activity 5

Although much of this vocabulary will already be familiar to students, reinforce it as follows. As you model each word, point to the corresponding part of your body. Next, make TPR commands for students to respond to, such as *Touch your foot* and *Point to your ankle.* Then point to parts of your body and have students name them. Finally, have students label the body parts on the figure in their books.

Activity 7

Refer to the procedure on page x.

As you introduce the vocabulary words, help students associate an illness or an organ with each one. For example, if you can't *breathe,* you may have a *cold.* If it hurts to *urinate,* you may have a problem with your *kidneys.*

Prepare students for the activities on pages 148 and 149 by asking these questions.

> *When you're sick and you have to go to the doctor, does the doctor always know what's wrong right away?; If the doctor doesn't know, what does he or she do?*

Activity 9

Before the listening activity, read through the health problems and have students repeat. Have them cover the columns labeled *Do tests?* and *Doctor's diagnosis* the first time they listen and uncover these columns on the second listening.

Activity 11

After students have completed the conversation and practiced it with their partners, have several pairs of students perform their dialogues for the class.

Activity 12

Before students fill out the form, go over it with them, explaining any terms they're unfamiliar with such as *insurance* and *allergies*.

Expansion Activity

To review *Wh-* questions in the past tense, have the class play "*Wh-* Question Bingo." (The only thing you'll need to prepare is lots of counters, coins, or little paper squares that students can use to cover up the squares on their bingo cards, which they will make in class.)

First, have the class brainstorm for as many *Wh-* expressions as they can think of. Write all of these expressions on the chalkboard. Then have each student draw a grid that is five squares across and five squares down. Tell students to write a *Wh-* expression above each of the five columns. Then put these verbs from Units 19, 20, and 21 on the chalkboard or project them onto a screen with an overhead projector.

open	deposit	shop	close	borrow	travel
gamble	return	look	chase	cook	do
live	pray	watch	use	visit	play
attend	study	go	see	eat	get
have	come	meet	sleep	leave	write
speak	tell	buy	drink	feel	make
ride	take	wear			

Have students choose 25 verbs from this list and fill in the squares on their bingo cards. It's important for students to understand that they are not to write the verbs in any particular order, since no two bingo cards should look the same. You may need to demonstrate how to do this by drawing two example bingo cards on the board. When students have finished their bingo cards, explain that when you call out a question, in order to cover a square on their bingo cards, they must have written the *Wh-* expression and the verb you use in the *same* column. You may need to ask a few example questions and refer to the bingo cards on the board to clarify this rule. Then begin the game. Call out *Wh-* questions containing the various verbs. For example:

How long did you *sleep*?

How much money did you *deposit*?

Write down the questions as you call them out. The first student to get five questions in a row or on the diagonal wins the game. Prizes may be awarded, but check for accuracy by comparing students' bingo cards with your notes before giving out the prizes. The game may be played several times.

UNIT 23 EXERCISES

A. Read Susan's note to Paul's teacher.

Dear Mrs. Adams,   April 15

      Paul can't come to school today or tomorrow because he was in an accident. He was playing in the street, and a car hit him. Our neighbor saw the accident and called an ambulance. We waited five minutes, but the ambulance didn't come. So we took Paul to the hospital ourselves. The doctor in the emergency room saw him **right away**. She took Paul's temperature and **blood pressure** and did some tests. Everything was fine except Paul's left wrist. His wrist was **broken**.

      Paul is staying home with me today and tomorrow. Next week, he'll return to school.

                                       Sincerely,
                                       Susan Gomez

B. Read the answers. Then write the questions.

1. <u>What happened to Paul yesterday?</u>

   A car hit him.

2. _____

   He was playing in the street.

3. _____

   He called an ambulance.

4. _____

   They waited five minutes.

5. _____

   He went to the hospital by car.

6. _____

   She took his temperature and blood pressure and did some tests.

7. _____

   It was broken.

8. _____

   He'll go back to school next week.

 **UNIT 24** # Yesterday, Today, and Tomorrow

Topic: travel

Life Skill/Competency: making reservations

Structure: tense review

Vocabulary

make reservations	lie in the sun	feel lonely	weigh himself
buy plane tickets	pack her suitcase	call Ken	feel bad
fly to Hawaii	kiss Ken good-bye	eat ice cream	go on a diet

Teaching Suggestions
Activity 1

Refer to the procedure on page v.

During the presentation, the focus should be on the new vocabulary. During the conversation practice (Activity 4), more attention can be given to proper tense selection.

Ask questions like the following to present the pictures.

What did (the Satos) do (two days ago)?

What (are they) doing right now?

What (are they) going to do tomorrow?

Why (is he/she) feeling _____?

Have/Do you ever _____?

When did/do you _____?

The following is a sample presentation of Picture 1 (the Satos making reservations).

> Let's see what's happening with our friends this week. You see, the Satos are taking a trip. But what did they do two days ago? Did they make hamburgers, or make reservations?...They made reservations. What does that mean?...Yes, you make reservations for your plane ticket. You call the airlines, and what do you tell them?...The day...and time...and place you're going. Also, they made reservations for what [pointing]?...Yes, they made reservations for their hotel. What do you say when you make hotel reservations?...Yes, what day you're going, and...how many people, and...how many nights you're staying. So the Satos made plane and hotel reservations two days ago.

Activity 4

Refer to the procedure on page ix.

As you practice the conversations with the students, remind them of the pronunciation of *going to* in informal speech, and encourage them to use it during the pairwork.

Grammar Box (page 154 of Student Book, top)

Refer to the procedure on page viii.

Have students brainstorm for a list of habitual activities they do during the day, such as *eat breakfast, read the newspaper, go to work, have a coffee break.* Write these activities on the chalkboard. Then ask a couple of students questions with *Did you already...?* and write the questions and their answers on the board. Help students recall the intonation patterns for yes/no questions and short answers and mark them with arrows. Then, in each of the questions, cross out the words *Did you* and above them write *Dija* (or *Diju*), as follows.

Dija
~~Did you~~ already read the newspaper?   Yes, I did.

Dija
~~Did you~~ already eat lunch?   No, I didn't.

Explain that *Did you* is often pronounced /dija/ or /diju/ in rapid speech. Have students repeat the questions and answers with the correct pronunciation and intonation. Then point to the activities on the list one by one and have students practice asking you questions. Respond with information about what you have and haven't done. Then call on pairs of students to ask and answer questions with *Did you*. Help them with pronunciation and intonation in their sentences.

Activity 5

After you model the conversations for the students, call their attention to the different verb tenses used in the questions. Point out that if the response to the second question, *Did you already...?*, is affirmative, the *when* question will be asked in the past tense. If the answer is negative, the *when* question will be asked in the future with *going to*.

Before students start the pairwork (with their books closed), write the question cues *How often?, Already?, and When?* and the verb phrases on the chalkboard.

Grammar Box (page 154 of Student Book, middle)

Refer to the procedure on page viii.

Ask several students to make statements about their activities using *already* and *not...yet*.

Activity 6

After students finish the writing task, have them share some of their sentences with the class.

For reinforcement of *Wh-* questions in the past tense, refer to the Expansion Activity.

Activity 7

Refer to the procedure on page x.

Prepare students for the activities on pages 155 and 156 by asking these questions.

If you want to go somewhere by plane, what do you have to do before you go?; Who do you have to call?; What do you have to tell the travel agent?; What does the travel agent tell you?

Activity 8

This listening task is demanding in that each airline reservation contains a lot of information for students to write down, so play the tape at least twice.

Activity 9

After students have completed the conversation and practiced it with their partners, have several pairs of students perform their dialogues for the class.

Activity 10

As students look at the information on flight arrivals and departures, ask for volunteers to point out the location of Boston, Chicago, Houston, and Seattle on a map of the United States. After students answer the questions, check their work by having students write the answers on the chalkboard.

Expansion Activity

For a challenging review of question formation in the simple present, present continuous, future with *going to*, and past tenses, make an overhead transparency of the following chart and have the students play *Jeopardy*. In addition to this transparency, you'll need 30 counters or squares of paper to cover the answers.

	HEALTH	HOUSING	BANK/POST OFFICE	EMERGENCIES	TRAVEL
25 POINTS	I have an earache.	I'm moving to Florida.	I opened a checking account.	She drank gasoline.	I'm leaving next week.
50 POINTS	Take two tablespoons twice a day.	They moved last March.	She's going to deposit $550.	It's on the corner of Market and 3rd Avenue.	We're going to stay for ten days.
75 POINTS	He called in sick.	Yes. I'd like service for my new apartment.	Yes, there is. The service charge is $4 a month.	He drank the whole bottle.	She's talking to a travel agent.
100 POINTS	I'm going to have the operation on Friday.	We pay gas and electricity.	Yes. I'd like a change of address form, please.	She's choking.	They go to Hawaii every summer.
150 POINTS	No, I don't. But I'm congested.	The payment is due on Dec. 15.	You can pick it up tomorrow after 10:00 A.M.	Yes. The driver is unconscious.	I want to leave on May 21 before noon.
200 POINTS	It started three days ago.	She owes $32.75 for service this month.	No, it wasn't. It was a large envelope.	Let's put some ice on his hand.	Yes, I did. I bought them last week.

To play the game, put the transparency on the overhead projector and cover all the answers with markers before turning on the projector. (If you don't have an overhead projector, the same chart can be drawn on the chalkboard and each question covered with a piece of paper.)

1. Divide the class into two or more teams and number the members of each team.

2. A member of one team chooses a topic and the number of points. (The more difficult questions are awarded a greater number of points.)

3. He or she must ask a question that corresponds to the answer for the topic and number of points chosen. If the answer contains the pronouns *he, she, it,* or *they,* the question should be formulated using an appropriate noun. For example, an appropriate question for *It opens at 9:00 A.M.* might be *When does the bank open?*

4. If a student asks an appropriate question, his or her team will be awarded the number of points to the left of the question. If a students asks a question that is not appropriate, a member of another team gets a chance to ask a question.

5. Keep score on the board.

6. When all of the answers have elicited appropriate questions, the game ends. The team with the most points wins.

A.   Read Judy's letter to Ken.

Dear Ken,   May 2
    Mexico City is a great place for a vacation! I'm having a wonderful time.
    Yesterday, I went shopping at the market. There were so many things to
look at! I didn't know what to buy. I used my credit card to get something
for you. Can you **guess** what it is?
    All that shopping made me tired, so today I'm relaxing at my hotel. I'm
sitting next to the swimming pool right now. This evening, I'm going dancing.
    Tomorrow, I'm going to see my friends Marta and Paulo. We're going to
visit a museum together. I **can't wait** to see them! I saw them last in 1992.
    Say hello to everyone at the bicycle factory. I don't miss work, but I
miss my friends there. And of course, I miss you.

                                                                          Love,
                                                                          Judy

**B.   Look at the pictures of Judy's activities in Mexico City and write *yesterday*,
today, or *tomorrow*.**

_____   _____   _____

_____   _____   _____

C.   Write sentences about Judy's activities in Mexico City.

1. <u>Yesterday, she</u> _____

2. _____

3. _____

4. _____

5. _____

6. _____

UNIT 25 What Should I Do Next?

Topic: job responsibilities

Life Skills/Competencies: requesting instructions; job benefits

Structure: modal *should* in questions

Vocabulary

Peel apples.	Use a knife.	Peel two pounds.	
Make boxes.	Use glue.	Make one dozen.	
Sew buttons.	Use a needle and thread.	Sew five buttons.	Use blue thread.
Paint the walls.	Use a paintbrush.	Paint the whole room.	Use white paint.
Wash windows.	Use a sponge.	Do the whole house.	
Fix chairs.	Use a screwdriver.	Fix four chairs.	
Wipe the cabinet.	Empty the wastebasket.	dental insurance	
Change the light bulb.	Weigh the package.	paid vacation	
Sweep the restroom.	benefits	paid holidays	
Put this in the drawer.	health insurance	sick days	

Teaching Suggestions
Activity 1

Refer to the procedure on page v.

Look at page 158 while presenting page 157, and introduce the language in the captions by asking about what is happening in each picture. Then, for each picture, ask the students for instructions—as though they were your supervisor at work—to elicit the language you have introduced. (See sample presentation below.) Students will not be formally introduced to—or asked to produce—questions with *should* until the conversation practice (page 159).

Ask the following questions to introduce each picture.

> What is the worker *doing*?
>
> What is he/she *using* to do the job?
>
> *How many* is he/she _____ing?
>
> *What color* is he/she using? [Pictures 3 and 4 only]

Then tell the students they are your supervisor. Ask the following questions for each picture.

> What should I *do* next?
>
> What should I *use* to _____?
>
> *How many* should I _____?
>
> *What color* _____ should I use? [Pictures 3 and 4 only]

The following is a sample presentation of Picture 1 (peeling apples).

> Today we're going to talk again about things people do at work. What's happening in this picture?...Is the person eating apples or peeling apples?...Yes, he's peeling apples. What else do we peel?...Yes, we peel bananas, and...oranges, and...sometimes we peel potatoes. Now, what's this guy using to peel the apples [pointing]?...He's using a knife. And how many apples is he peeling?...Two pounds. Now, let's practice. I'm the worker and you're my supervisor, OK? Tell me, boss, what should I do next [pointing]?...OK. And what should I use to peel them?...All right. And how many should I peel? Got it! Now, class, let's look at the next picture...

Grammar Box (page 159 of Student Book)

Refer to the procedure on page viii.

Have a box of colored chalk and two dolls or puppets on hand to use when presenting the new structure. First, with white chalk, write the following cues on the chalkboard.

What/do

How many

What/use

What color

Next, using the dolls or puppets, say the following dialogue.

A: What should I do?

B: Write the names of vegetables.

A: How many should I write?

B: Four.

A: What should I use to write them?

B: Use chalk.

A: What color chalk should I use?

B: Pink.

A: Got it!

Then make it appear as though Doll/Puppet A is following the instructions by writing the names of four vegetables on the board with pink chalk. Put the dolls away and model the dialogue again, having students repeat.

To continue the practice, the class will take Part A and you will take Part B. Call on individual students to listen and follow instructions. Cue the questions from the class by pointing to the cues on the board. In your instructions, vary the number of things you ask students to write on the board and the color of the chalk they write with. Your instructions may include writing the names of things like these: body parts, businesses, organs, occupations, health problems, sports, utilities, furniture.

Activity 5

After students finish the writing task, have them practice their dialogues with a partner. Then ask several pairs of students to perform their dialogues for the class.

Activity 6

Present all six pictures by introducing the language in the box at the bottom of page 160 in the same way you introduced the language on page 158. (Each sentence corresponds to the picture with the same number.) Tell your students again that they are your supervisor. Point to the pictures one by one and ask, *What should I do now, boss?*, thus eliciting the instructions you have just introduced. This time, however, ask a clarification question (suggested clearly by each picture) in response to each instruction from the students.

Instruction (from student)	Your clarification question
1. Wipe the cabinet.	You mean the inside or the outside?
2. Change the light bulb.	You mean the left one or the right one?
3. Sweep the restroom.	You mean the men's room or the women's room?
4. Put this in the drawer.	You mean the top one or the bottom one?
5. Empty the wastebasket.	You mean the tall one or the short one?
6. Weigh the package.	You mean the big one or the little one?

(Your "supervisors" can answer your clarification questions as they wish.)

Activity 7

Before students begin the conversation practice, point out and model the intonation pattern indicated by the arrows in the box below the pictures.

Grammar Box (page 160 of Student Book)

Refer to the procedure on page viii.

Encourage more practice with the intonation pattern indicated by the arrows in the box. Help students recall that in choice questions, the voice goes up on the first choice and down on the second choice. Write the following cues and arrows on the chalkboard.

inside/outside↘   left one/right one↘   men's room/women's room↘

top one/bottom one↘   tall one/short one↘   big one/little one↘

Give the instructions cued by each picture in Activity 6 and have students ask for clarification using the cues on the chalkboard. Help them with intonation. Before students go on to Activity 7, erase the cues from the board.

For more practice requesting instructions and asking for clarification, refer to Expansion Activity 1.

Activity 8

Refer to the procedure on page x.

As you present the vocabulary for each benefit, ask if anyone in the class has that type of benefit through their job. If so, have the student attempt to explain what it is. Clarify as necessary.

Activity 10

After students have completed the conversation and practiced it with their partners, have two pairs of students perform it for the class.

Activity 11

After students have asked their partners about the different types of benefits they get through their jobs, ask students if there are other benefits they receive that are not presented in this unit. If so, write these benefits on the chalkboard and have students explain what they are.

For reinforcement of job benefits, refer to Expansion Activity 2.

Expansion Activities

1. Reinforce and expand on requesting and following instructions at work by having students do role-plays. Put students in pairs and hand each pair a notecard (which you have made before class) with phrases like these.

make some bread	fix the pipes	sew pants
make some cookies	fix the doors	sew T-shirts
make some salads	fix the electricity	sew skirts
serve the drinks	clean the rugs	wash the pots and pans
serve the ice cream	clean the floors	wash the silverware
serve the cake	clean the mirrors	wash the cups
peel the potatoes	paint the tables	weigh the letters
peel the oranges	paint the bookshelves	weigh the packages
peel the carrots	paint the cabinets	weigh the boxes

Have each pair of students write a dialogue that begins *What should I do next?* and follows the pattern of the model dialogues on page 159 of the Student Book. Have students practice these dialogues with their partners and then perform them for the class.

2. Review job benefits with a mingling activity in which students move around the room asking their classmates questions. Pass out copies of (or have students copy from the chalkboard) the following form.

Find 3 people who get sick days at work.	Find 3 people who get paid holidays.
1. _____	1. _____
2. _____	2. _____
3. _____	3. _____
Find 3 people who get health insurance.	Find 3 people who get dental insurance.
1. _____	1. _____
2. _____	2. _____
3. _____	3. _____

Before starting the activity, read the instructions with the students and model the task. Circulate and ask several students if they get sick days at work. Write on your form the names of those who answer in the affirmative. Remind students to use the correct intonation for yes/no questions (rising) and short answers (rising/falling). Then have all students stand up and begin interviewing their classmates.

A. **Read the job announcements.**

Construction Worker	Factory Worker	Secretary/Receptionist
Medium-sized construction co. needs supervisor for 10-man construction crew. Exp. req. Must speak English and Spanish. Must have trucker's license. Benefits: • medical and dental • 2 weeks' paid vacation To apply, call Briggs Construction Co. at 345-2009. Ask for Mr. Leader.	Shoe factory has full-time, temp. opening on night shift. No exp. nec. Sal. $9/hour. Overtime $13.50/hour. Benefits: • health insurance Apply in person to Beale Shoe Factory, 1255 Barnett St. Ask for Mrs. Page.	Large advertising co. looking for full-time front desk person. Must speak English and Chinese, have good phone skills, and know how to use computers. Starting sal. $2,000/mo. Benefits: • medical and dental • paid holidays Apply in person to Woo Advertising, 644 West 3rd. Ave., Suite 902.

B. **Read the sentences. Write *construction worker, factory worker*, or *secretary/receptionist*. Sometimes you will write two jobs.**

1. You have to speak Chinese. <u>secretary/receptionist</u>

2. No experience is necessary. _____

3. You should go to the employer to apply. _____

   _____

4. You get paid vacation. _____

5. You get paid for working overtime. _____

6. You get dental insurance. _____

7. You have to know how to drive a truck. _____

8. You get a monthly salary. _____

9. You work at night. _____

10. You get paid holidays. _____

11. You should call the employer to apply. _____

12. You must know how to use a computer. _____

You Should Never Do That!

Topic: job safety

Life Skill/Competency: paycheck stubs

Structure: modal *should(n't)*

Vocabulary You should never bend over to pick up something heavy. You might hurt your back.
You should always wear gloves when you hold glass. You might cut your hands.
You should never smoke near gasoline. You might start a fire.
You should always carry scissors pointing down. You might hurt somebody.
You should never touch electrical wires. You might get a shock.
You should always wear safety glasses around machines. You might hurt your eyes.

regular pay   gross pay   federal tax   F.I.C.A.

overtime pay   take-home pay   state tax   union dues

Teaching Suggestions

(The final activity in this unit requires that students bring in a pay stub from their own, a family member's, or a friend's paycheck. Inform students of this in advance of the day you plan to have them work on Activity 10 of the Student Book so they can be prepared.)

Activity 1

Refer to the procedure on page v.

Look at page 164 while presenting page 163, and introduce the language by asking these two questions about each picture.

What's the problem?

Why isn't this safe?

Clarify the meanings of *should never, should always,* and *might* as you introduce them. Reinforce the new vocabulary by relating it to your students' lives, as in the sample presentation for Picture 1 (bending over to pick up something heavy).

> Today we're going to talk about safety on the job. What's "safety"?...Yes, it means you are safe. Does that mean you have an accident?...No. Safety means you don't have accidents. Look at this person. What's he doing?...Yes, he's picking something up. Is it light or heavy?...It's heavy. And how is he doing that [demonstrating]?...He's bending over. For example, when do we bend over?...When we drop something or...when we tie our shoes. Is it a good idea to bend over when we pick up something heavy?...No, it isn't. We should never bend over to pick up something heavy. What do I mean, "should never"?...Yes, it means it's not a good idea. And why shouldn't we bend over to pick up heavy things? Because we might...yes, we might hurt our back. What do I mean, "might"?...Yes, "maybe." If we pick up something this way, maybe we'll hurt our back.

Grammar Box (page 165 of Student Book)

Refer to the procedure on page viii.

Write *never* and *always* on the chalkboard. Cue students with verb phrases and have them make sentences using *You should never...* and *You should always....* Then ask them to state a reason with *might.* For example:

T: Walk alone at night.

Ss: You should never walk alone at night.

T: Why not?

Ss: Because someone might hurt you.

Here are some other phrases you can use to cue students.

leave your car unlocked	eat fruit and vegetables	brush your teeth
drive too fast	play in the street	come to class on time
register for class early	give candy to a baby	argue with your boss
wear slippers at home	stand outside in the rain	get lots of exercise

For reinforcement of language related to safety, refer to Expansion Activity 1.

Activity 5

After students finish the writing task, have them share some of their sentences with the class.

Activity 6

Write the warnings in the box on the chalkboard. Model each warning and have students tell you which syllable is louder. Mark the stressed syllable with a dot.

Look out!   Watch it!   Careful!   Slow down!

Model each warning and have students repeat as necessary, stressing the correct syllable.

As you look at the pictures and read the signs with the students, have them describe what they see and what's going on in each picture.

For more practice with warnings, refer to Expansion Activity 2.

Activity 7

Prepare students for the activities on pages 167 and 168 by asking the following questions.

How often do you get paid?; Do you get a pay stub with your paycheck?; What information is on the pay stub?; Are you a member of a union? Do you pay union dues?; Do you keep your pay stub or throw it away? Why?

Before students start scanning the paycheck for answers to the questions, explain the difference between *regular (hours/pay)* and *overtime (hours/pay),* and the difference between *gross pay* and *net pay.* Also, explain the meaning of the word *deductions,* and briefly discuss the different deductions printed on the pay stub. As students are looking for answers to the questions, circulate to further explain unfamiliar vocabulary and to show them where to find answers they can't locate themselves. After students have had ample time to write the answers, have volunteers write them on the chalkboard.

Activity 8

Before you read about figuring paychecks with the students, do some simple math operations on the chalkboard to verify that students understand how to add, subtract, and multiply numbers. Introduce the words *plus, minus, times,* and *equals,* and have students read some simple equations aloud, such as *One plus one equals two.*

Activity 9

After students have worked with their partners to write answers to the questions, check their work by having volunteers write the answers on the chalkboard.

For reinforcement of language related to paychecks, refer to Expansion Activity 3.

Expansion Activities

1. Review the vocabulary for unsafe actions by miming the actions presented on page 163. (You'll need a pair of scissors and some wire as props.) Write the following cues for a dialogue on the chalkboard.

    A: Hey! That's dangerous!

    B: _____?

    A: You should _____.

    B: _____?

    A: Because _____.

    Mime the unsafe actions one by one. Have students warn you not to do those things and offer reasons why. Then mime sticking your finger in an electrical outlet, trying to move something that's very heavy (such as a file cabinet), throwing things down on the floor, and walking barefoot across the room. Help students make warnings and offer reasons why these actions are dangerous.

2. Make some large warning signs, like those pictured at the bottom of page 166, and post them at different places around the classroom. Point to them one by one and have students read them aloud. Then put students in pairs. Have them write short dialogues in which one person tells another not to do something based on one of the warnings posted on the wall. Have students practice their dialogues aloud and perform them in front of the class, using the appropriate warning signs as props.

3. Give students additional practice with vocabulary related to paychecks. Dictate the following problem for students to write.

    Last week, Judy worked overtime.

    She worked 40 hours at $9 an hour.

    She worked six hours at $13.50 an hour.

    Her taxes came to $132.

    Her insurance was $25.

    What was Judy's take-home pay?

    Have students work in pairs to solve the problem. When they have finished, ask a student to write the mathematical operations on the chalkboard.

A. **Read the letter from Paul's grandmother.**

Dear Paul,   May 15
    How are you now? I hope you're feeling better. Your mother wrote me
about the accident. What a scary thing!
    Here are some things to remember when you play outside. You should
never play in the street. Cars go fast, and a car might hit you again. At
your house, you have a nice yard. You should play in the yard. If your ball
goes into the street, you shouldn't run after it. You should call your sister,
Linda. She can get it for you. If Linda isn't there, you should call your mom
or dad. And when you ride your bicycle, ride only on the sidewalk. Never
ride in the street.
    It's nice to play with your friends. It's nice to be friendly with your
neighbors. But you should be careful of strangers. Never get into a
stranger's car.
    Your mother says you're back in school now. I'm happy to hear that!
I hope you're having lots of fun.

                                                                                    Love,
                                                                                    Grandma

B. **Write the things Paul should and shouldn't do.**

should

He should play in the yard.

_____

_____

_____

_____

shouldn't

_____

_____

_____

_____

UNIT 27 Is Your Hometown Rainy?

Topic: your hometown
Life Skill/Competency: invitations
Structure: comparatives
Vocabulary

rainy	quiet	live in the city	get up early
hilly	clean	live in the country	sleep late
cold	safe	walk	read
windy	busy	take the bus	watch TV
big	friendly	eat out	go out
old	cheap	eat at home	stay home

Teaching Suggestions
Activity 1

Refer to the procedure on page v.

Before beginning the presentation, write the word *compare* and the ending *-er* on the chalkboard, and tell students that we use *-er* to compare. Establish the meaning of *compare* with a few simple examples: Have two students stand, and say *Tran is taller;* point to a young student and say *I am older,* and so forth. Elicit only short answers during the presentation; students will not be asked to produce comparative statements or questions until they are introduced on pages 171 and 172.

Ask questions like the following to present the pictures on page 169.

Do you like _____ cities?

Do you know a city/country that's very _____?

Is your hometown _____?

Is our city _____?

Which is _____er, your hometown or our city?

(A little _____er or a lot _____er?)

The following is a sample presentation of Picture 1 (rainy).

> Today we're going to talk about your hometown and our city. Do you like rainy cities [pointing to the picture]?...You don't, Javier? How come?...Oh, you always have to carry your umbrella in rainy places...And sometimes your shoes get wet when it's rainy. Do you know a place that's very rainy?...Hong Kong is rainy in June...and Seattle is rainy. What about your hometown, Ali? Is it rainy there?...Not very rainy. What about you, Chau? Which is rainier, your hometown or our city?...Your hometown is rainier. Is it a little rainier or a lot rainier?...Oh, it's a lot rainier.

Grammar Box (page 171 of Student Book, top)

Refer to the procedure on page viii.

Call students' attention to the intonation pattern indicated by the arrows in the box. Help them recall that in choice questions, the voice goes up on the first choice and down on the second choice. Point out that the voice also goes down on the comparative adjective. Supply cues, such as *cold, quiet, friendly,* and so forth, and have students make choice questions using the comparative form of the adjectives.

Activity 4

Remind students to use the correct intonation as they practice the conversations with you and do the pairwork with their partners.

Grammar Boxes (page 171 of Student Book, middle)

Refer to the procedure on page viii.

Explain that while the comparative of many adjectives is formed according to the four spelling patterns exemplified in the first box, the second box contains three common adjectives with irregular comparative forms.

Activity 5

If additional practice spelling the comparative forms of adjectives is necessary, have students copy the following adjectives from the chalkboard and write their comparative forms.

low	weak	deep
high	white	wide
heavy	dark	dirty
fat	red	gray
thin	pretty	tiny
strong	ugly	slim

Grammar Box (page 172 of Student Book, top)

Refer to the procedure on page viii.

Have a world map to refer to. Show students where you're from by pointing to the place on the map. Then supply adjective cues and have students ask you questions about your hometown and the city where you live now. Respond appropriately.

Activity 6

Before students start the pairwork, have several of them come forward and point to their hometowns on the world map.

Grammar Box (page 172 of Student Book, middle)

Refer to the procedure on page viii.

Have a large map of the United States to refer to. Ask students which U.S. cities and states they have visited and have them point to these cities and states on the map. Ask individual students to compare cities and states they're familiar with to the city and state where they now live. For example:

        T: New York and Florida, José.

        J: New York is colder than Florida.

Activity 7

After students finish the writing task, have them share some of their sentences with the class.

For reinforcement of comparative adjectives, refer to Expansion Activity 1.

Activity 8

Refer to the cues in the box at the bottom of the page during your presentation. Ask these questions to present each picture.

Which do you like better/more, _____ing or _____ing?

Why do you like _____ing more?

Grammar Box (page 173 of Student Book)

Refer to the procedure on page viii.

Have students brainstorm for a list of sports and leisure activities, and write these activities on the chalkboard, (e.g., *go shopping, swim,* and *play tennis*). Using the activities on this list, model a couple of choice questions, using the correct intonation. Call students' attention to the arrows in the box. In addition, point out that the choices must be stated with the *-ing* form of verbs. Call on individual students to ask you which activities you like better; respond appropriately. After you've responded to a number of questions, have students ask other questions of their classmates. Help them with intonation.

For reinforcement of choice questions, refer to Expansion Activity 2.

Activity 11

After students have practiced inviting their partners to do the activities pictured at the bottom of the page, have several pairs of students perform their conversations for the class.

For more practice with invitations, refer to Expansion Activity 3.

Expansion Activities

1. Review the adjectives presented on pages 169 and 172 and reinforce comparatives. First, hold up flashcards (which you have made before class) with the adjectives and have students read them aloud. Then have three or four students use each adjective in a sentence comparing two places they know (e.g., *Singapore is noisier than Seattle*).

2. Review questions with *Which do you like better?* First, ask this question using the vocabulary from page 173. Then write the following topics on the chalkboard: *sports, work, housing, shopping, food,* and *travel*. Tell students to use the topics on the chalkboard as cues as they write six choice questions for their partners. Point to the different topics as you offer some examples.

   Which do you like better, running or playing tennis?; Which do you like better, paying with cash or using a credit card?; Which do you like better, working the day shift or working the night shift?

   After students have written their questions, have them interview their partners and note their responses. Then have them write six sentences about their partners' preferences. Write the following example sentences on the board.

   Marta likes using her credit card more than paying with cash.

   Lan likes running more than playing tennis.

   When the students have finished their sentences, collect their papers.

3. Strip Story. Using the dialogues on page 174 as models, type out two new dialogues and cut them into strips of paper, with one strip per line of text. Put students into pairs and give each pair all of the strips necessary to create the dialogues. (The strips should not be in order.) Ask students to arrange the strips to create two conversations. Then have them practice the conversations aloud.

A. Oakland and San Francisco are two cities in California. They're near each other, but they have some differences. Read about the two cities.

	OAKLAND	SAN FRANCISCO
Age	founded 1854	founded 1850
Population	372,242 people	723,959 people
Average Personal Income	$22,249/year	$28,170/year
Average Temperature	Jan.– 49°/July–63.7°	Jan.– 48.5°/July–62.2°
Weather	sunny	cloudy and windy
Description	flat	hilly

B. Write sentences comparing Oakland and San Francisco. Use the words in the box.

big	cloudy	cold	flat	hilly
old	poor	sunny	warm	windy

1. <u>San Francisco is cloudier than Oakland.</u>

2. _____

3. _____

4. _____

5. _____

6. _____

7. _____

8. _____

9. _____

10. _____

UNIT 28 Is Your Hometown Crowded?

Topic: your hometown
Life Skill/Competency: compliments
Structure: comparatives
Vocabulary   crowded   expensive   famous
                beautiful   dangerous   interesting
                modern   scenic   fun

Teaching Suggestions
Activity 1

Refer to the procedure on page v.

Before beginning the presentation, tell students that we sometimes use *more* to compare. (The rule for using *-er* or *more* will be formally presented on page 177.) Elicit short answers during the presentation.

Ask questions like the following to present the pictures.

> Do you like _____ cities?
>
> Do you know a city/country that's very _____?
>
> Is your hometown _____?
>
> Is our city _____?
>
> Which is more _____, your hometown or our city?
>
> (A lot more _____ or a little more _____?)

The following is a sample presentation of Picture 1 (crowded).

> Today we're going to talk some more about your hometown and our city. Do you like cities that are crowded [pointing to the picture]?...Looks like you don't. What does it mean when a city is crowded?...Yes, it means a lot of people close together. For example, where is it crowded in our city?...It's crowded on the buses. Where else?...It's crowded in Chinatown. What about your hometown, Sandra? Is it very crowded?...It isn't. Abdullah, which is more crowded, your hometown or our city?...Your hometown. Well, is it a lot more crowded or just a little more crowded?...Oh, it's a lot more crowded.

Grammar Box (page 177 of Student Book, top)

Refer to the procedure on page viii.

Write four single-syllable adjectives in one column and four multisyllable adjectives (not ending in *-y)* in another column on the chalkboard. Clap the syllables as you model the adjectives. Have students tell you the number of syllables each adjective has. Then ask students to attempt to derive the rule for forming comparative adjectives. Explain that while single-syllable adjectives are made into comparatives by adding *-er,* multisyllable adjectives must be preceded by *more.* Point out that one exception to the rule is multisyllable adjectives ending in *-y,* and another exception is the adjective *fun,* whose comparative form is *more fun.* Then supply cues with multisyllable adjectives such as *beautiful, modern,* and *famous* and have students ask you questions about your hometown and the city where you live now. Remind them to use the correct intonation, and respond appropriately to their questions.

Activity 4

Before you practice the conversation with the students, write the first exchange on the chalkboard and review intonation in choice questions and answers. Model the exchange, and have students tell you the intonation patterns. Mark the intonation with arrows.

Which is more scenic, your hometown or this city?

My hometown.

Model the second exchange in like manner. Have students repeat, using the correct intonation.

Grammar Box (page 177 of Student Book, middle)

Refer to the procedure on page viii.

Cue students with the names of two cities, states, or countries they're likely to be familiar with and have them make sentences containing the comparative forms of multisyllable adjectives. For example:

> T: Hong Kong and San Diego, Suhua.
>
> S: Hong Kong is more interesting than San Diego.

Activity 5

After students finish the writing task, have them share some of their sentences with the class.

For reinforcement of comparative adjectives, refer to Expansion Activities 1 and 2.

Activity 6

Refer to the procedure on page x.

Prepare students for the activities on page 178 by asking these questions.

> *If you like someone's new clothes, what do you sometimes say?; Do you give people compliments often?; What things can you give people compliments about?; How do you respond to compliments?*

Activity 8

Before students start the pairwork, suggest that they use the dialogue at the top of Student Book page 178 as a guide for their conversations. Model the task by offering compliments to two or three students in the class. For example:

> T: I really like your sweater, Ping.
>
> P: Thank you.
>
> T: It's so colorful. Is it warm?
>
> P: Yes, it is. It's warmer than my jacket.

For more practice with compliments, refer to Expansion Activity 3.

Expansion Activities

1. Review and contrast the comparative forms of the adjectives presented in Units 27 and 28. First, hold up flashcards (which you have made before class) with the adjectives presented in both units and have students read them aloud. Then have three or four students use each adjective in a sentence comparing two places they know (e.g., *San Francisco is more famous than Santa Fe*).

2. Continue the review of comparative adjectives by writing the following cues on the chalkboard.

   boots/slippers/expensive

   trains/city buses/crowded

   classes at the university/classes at this school/cheap

   my boss/my landlord/friendly

   motorcycles/bicycles/dangerous

   chopsticks/knives and forks/easy to use

   my house in the United States/my house in my country/modern

   camping in the mountains/going to the beach/fun

   the moon/the sun/big

   love stories/funny movies/interesting

   Have students write sentences using these cues. After they've finished writing, have them share some of their sentences with the class and then hand in their papers.

3. Have students brainstorm for a list of things we offer people compliments on, such as hairstyles, houses, cars, and photos. Write this list on the chalkboard. Then put students in pairs and have each pair of students write three dialogues similar to the model on page 178 in which one student offers a compliment and the other responds with a sentence containing a comparative adjective. After students have finished writing, give them time to practice the dialogues. Then have several pairs of students perform one of their dialogues for the class.

A. Read Judy's letter to her friend Debbie.

Dear Debbie,   June 16

    I'm back from Mexico City, and I had a wonderful time. Guess what?
I'm already planning my vacation for next summer! But I can't decide.
Should I go to New York or Hawaii?

    New York is a big city. Of course, it's crowded and noisy. It's expensive,
and some areas are dangerous too. But New York is very interesting. There
are so many things to do. You can visit museums and go to movies. You
can eat great food in restaurants.

    On the other hand, Hawaii is very beautiful. The mountains and the
beaches are scenic. And the weather in Hawaii is great. It's warm and
sunny all the time. The people are friendly too.

    Where will I have more fun? I don't know. Tell me what you think.

Love,
Judy

B. Write sentences comparing New York and Hawaii. Use the words in the box.

beautiful	crowded	dangerous	expensive	friendly
interesting	noisy	scenic	sunny	warm

   1. <u>New York is more crowded than Hawaii.</u>

   2. _____

   3. _____

   4. _____

   5. _____

   6. _____

   7. _____

   8. _____

   9. _____

  10. _____